Schopenhauer's Critique of Hope

DR. ORTRUN SCHULZ, born 1960 in Hannover, Germany. Master of Arts in Philosophy and English 1986, 1993 doctoral degree in Philosophy.
From 1992 until 2005 editor of the *Schopenhauer-Jahrbuch*. Private research and many trips abroad.

Hope is at the core of human existence. It can either be an emotion or an attitude. In either case, it is a natural and basic affection of the mind. This analysis of hope will clarify the concept by dealing with its involvement in knowledge, ethics and metaphysics. Hope can lead to truth or error, depending on whether it is a presentation of probabilities by the intellect, or just a reflection of expectations from the will. In this book, a short survey of views on hope, from the history of philosophy, will be followed by an account of Schopenhauer's critical approach. Hope will be treated within his framework of optimism and pessimism, and of how it may serve as an important element in the critique of ideologies.

Ortrun Schulz

Schopenhauer's Critique of Hope

© 2014 Ortrun Schulz

Printing and production: BoD - Books on Demand
GmbH, Norderstedt, Germany

ISBN 978-3-7357-5710-4

"[...] our Schopenhauer: he had no hope, but he wanted the truth."

(Friedrich Nietzsche, *Kritische Gesamt-Ausgabe*, ed. Giorgio Colli and Mazzino Montinari, Berlin/New York 1967 ff., 3,1, Aph. 20, p. 127. Transl. O.S.)

Contents

Preface

A critique of hope in our culture is probably not only well timed but even timeless, since the craving for a self-determined life in dignity and the hope to be affirmed in one's peculiar way of being in the world, is natural to man, and there is nobody whose hopes and dreams would never get more or less disappointed. The pursuit of happiness is always compromised. The slogan 'think big, think positive' is popular, as is the opinion that everybody is the master of one's happiness. In view of such ideas disappointments are considered as failures and they are felt like wounds. Therefore hope plays an important role in every theory of happiness. In the history of philosophy the value of hope is regarded as ambivalent.

Arthur Schopenhauer's predecessor Immanuel Kant wrote three critiques as answers to human basic questions: the *Critique of Pure Reason* answers the question, "what can we know?", the *Critique of Practical Reason* answers the question "what shall we do?", the *Critique of Judgment* treats the topic of the beautiful and the sublime, and the *Religion within the Limits of Pure Reason* answers the question "what may we hope?" As a matter of fact, hope proves to be an ingredient of all of these realms, which makes it obvious how useful a critique of hope is.

9

Schopenhauer is introduced as a representative of a critique of hope because of his interesting approach in this direction. In addition to a clarification and analysis of the term we shall also be looking at an evaluation. Schopenhauer reflects on the essence and objects of hope in his theory of happiness. Although he insists that only need is positively felt, and happiness is merely the absence of need, he is not definitely opposed to happiness. But the insatiable longing for happiness is a torture and springs from desire. Schopenhauer does not crush all hope. Instead he points out that the justified types of hope must be distinguished from those which lack justification. This is the meaning of 'critique'.

We shall reflect on the *conditions of objectivity* and the *conditions of invulnerability*. This presentation is more a theoretical analysis than a practical guide. Whether it is at all possible to control one's hopes depends on the answer to the question whether man can want what he would like to want, and this question cannot be answered with certainty. While there is little hope solving this mystery of free will, there is some hope that an analysis of hope will add to a better understanding of human existence. A critique of hope should be a contribution to wisdom.

This book was originally written in German in 2002 but after it got much positive feedback I decided to revise and translate it into English to make it available to speakers of English, too. My writing style would have been quite awkward if the manuscript had not been proofread by Jay Kendall, to whom I would like to extend my deep gratitude here.

Ortrun Schulz, Hannover (Germany) 2014

Introduction

Hope is an anthropological category. As wishful thinking, hope sheds light on an essential trait of human nature, his struggle for happiness. Hope is life's promise of happiness. Thinking clings almost like a reflex to what is uplifting, pleasant and agreeable. Human existence is permeated with hope. The analysis of the *conditio humana* reveals the struggle for goals along the way of the fundamental aim for self-preservation. There are needs and wants, and possible ways to meet them or not. These relations usually involve problems which are mentally represented as various states between security and doubt, hope and despair. Taken in the context of our existence, talking about hope involves questions of truth and error, optimism, pessimism and realism, will and intellect, desire, probability and expectation.

A distinction must be made between the act of hoping and the object of hope. Moreover, hope can either be a sudden affect, or a lasting attitude, as in the case of a passion. It can even be an act or voluntary decision. In the history of ideas, hope is often ranked among the passions which are regarded as leaving the subject passive, and which are just happening. However, sometimes an active participation of the subject in shaping the cognitive contents of hope must be taken into account also.

13

The object classes can be divided into world immanent and transcendent. In religion hope plays an important role as a promised good in the afterlife. The ethical individual is inclined to cherish hope for justice, if not in this life, then at least in an afterlife. For this purpose he must not only postulate a moral government of the world, but also hope for the immortality of the soul. Hell as described by Dante says, "Justice has brought me into being."

Some secular thought (for example Marxist theory and notions of utopia) shifts such transcendent hopes for heaven to expectations for paradise on earth.[1]

Hope can be more or less well-founded. Schopenhauer remarks that hope is a condition where the two aspects of our essence are competing against each other, namely will and intellect. The will is wanting its object, the intellect is estimating its probability. The larger the part of the will is, and the smaller the part of the intellect, the more fuel there is for hope; in the reverse case the less.[2]

Hope makes us vulnerable. Disappointment hurts, and therefore hope has often been considered as an evil in ancient theories of happiness. Within a theory of knowledge, the question arises how to determine possible reasons for hope. It becomes evident that the concept and criticism of hope must be addressed within any project linked to enlightenment. The attempt to pinpoint the components of hope and lay out the realm, as well as the limits, of hope is part of a critique of any ideology. Ideology misses reality, if what is advocated is subjectively considered as more probable than can be supported objectively by reasons.

A belief or belief system is not always limited to an individual and his or her stream of consciousness, but often has an outbound dimension, whenever it is communicated to others who are influenced by it. Like other ideas, hope can be encouraged or discouraged, it can spread to other people, who may rely and act on these grounds. In this case, more responsibility is incurred than when just dealing with oneself.

1. Traditional Views of Hope

In Greek antiquity the term of "hope" (*elpis*) corresponds roughly to "expectation". It refers to an unspecific future dimension.

Skeptical or even negative connotations concerning expectation are expressed by Pindar and Hesiod. They do not have high esteem of its subjective bias. Pindar mentions the "envious and greedy expectations of the mortals", which are nothing but selfish imaginations. Hesiod talks about "empty hope" or the futility of an optimistic expectation, for which no effort is made, and which is likely to eventually turn out to have been an illusion.

The ambivalence as to whether hope should be considered a plague or a good is reflected in the various versions of the *Pandora fable*. According to *Hesiod*, Zeus sends Pandora to earth with a jar filled with *evils*, and they all get released except the last one, hope. But in the version of *Babrius*, the jar contains *goods*, which all escape and only one, hope, is retained as consolation for man. Schopenhauer suspects that originally the jar contained goods as reported by Babrius and that the myth was either misunderstood or deliberately changed by Hesiod.[3]

The uncertainty of the future and the randomness of events, without obvious relation to human wishes and fates, result in a rather skeptical attitude towards hope, especially in the tragic poetry and Stoicism of Aeschylus and Sophocles.

Distinct from this, however, there is also an emphasis on a rational justification for assuming a desirable course of future events. Herodotus and Thucydides consider a well- founded hopeful assumption to be legitimate. Democritus distinguishes between the correct prognoses made by people with insight, and the impossible expectations of ignorant people.[4]

A merely probable prognosis, however, is not necessarily grounds for an expectation of a happy ending, as is typical for hope. This meaning, "a trust in positive future possibilities guided by subjective interest", can be found for the first time in Sophocles.

So we have discovered three main aspects of the meaning of "expectation" in archaic and classical antiquity:
1. Illusionary belief
2. Rational prognosis
3. Existential trust.[5]

Different views are also held by Plato and Aristotle. Plato calls hope, desire and anticipation the soul's grips on future things, differentiating between good and bad, true and false expectations. Schopenhauer ascribes to Plato having called "hope the dream of him who is awake."[6] Plato fosters a concept of hope which transcends the sensual world, and reaches its true destination only in the world of pure ideas, in view of the true, the beautiful and the good. This meaning is also included in Hellenistic and late antique religion.

Aristotle emphasizes the rational aspect of expectation, and describes a "science of prognosis." Like *fear*, he also considers hope as an *affection*. Fear is a depressed state; hope an uplifted state of the soul..[7]

In the *Old Testament* the concept of expectation clearly has the meaning of hope regarding the promised– good – future. Unlike the Greek rational prognosis, in the sense of an extrapolation from the present and its conditions, Jewish hope aims faithfully above reality at an eschatology, or end of time - the coming of the Messiah, the kingdom of God. Prudence advises to "avoid catching the wind" (Koheleth).

Christian hope is defined by the apostle Paul as "trust in God who raises the dead".

For Augustine hope means neither an uncertain expectation, nor hope for a future worldly good, but a transcendent one. Christianity adopts a strong tendency to "live so that it does not make sense anymore to live", as Friedrich Nietzsche puts it. The meaning of life becomes to live so that one merits a place in Heaven, or at least to make oneself worthy of God's grace. Augustine lists hope, together with faith and love, as the cardinal Christian virtues or commandments.

In the Christian Middle Ages the act of hoping (*spes qua*) is distinguished from the goal of hope (*spes quae*). The former is an affect which contains a pleasurable expectation of a future reality and has different degrees of intensity and certainty.[8]

Thomas Aquinas describes hope as a "striving motion", directed towards a possible future good.[9]

In Dante's *Divine Comedy* (1472) a line "in dark letters" at the entrance to hell reads: "Give up hope all ye enter here."[10] This suggests that hopelessness is the entrance to hell. The sinners' souls are condemned to remain restless forever: "No hope will give them strength to gain peace of mind or ease their pain."[11]

Martin Luther points out the difference between the general human hope in regard to an actual situation, and Christian hope growing from the believer's faith.

In the 17th and 18th century hope and fear are grouped together, and are treated within the theories of affects and politics, such as those of Thomas Hobbes, René Descartes und Baruch Spinoza. Hobbes mentions in his main work *Leviathan* that men can be manipulated by hope and fear.

As long as the intellect receives impressions, it remains passive. The term "passion" reveals this etymology. Descartes observes that the mere thought of a good within our reach would be stimulus enough for us to desire it. If we believe in a sufficient probability of obtaining it, then we are filled with hope. If hope becomes strong enough, its nature changes, and is called "confidence."[12]

Hope may involve a false judgment. Unwarranted hope is an error which results from one's will or faculty of affirmation expanding further than what the intellect understands clearly and distinctly. Overriding passions make us slaves and should be overcome. Descartes claims there is a freedom of the will and unrestricted power of mind over the affections. While Blaise Pascal allows for "reasons of the heart" in faith, René Descartes advises to doubt everything first, in order to then gain certain knowledge, similar to that in mathematics.

His follower Baruch Spinoza claims the strife for self-preservation as basic principle and origin of all affects. According to him this force is the essence of man, as well as everything else. Man tends to imagine pleasant things as real.[13] He defines hope as an unstable joy, resulting from an idea of some future or past thing, in an outcome about which we are in doubt.[14] Due to uncertainty in our reflection on this outcome's degree of probability, both the affections of joy and sadness are involved. This oscillating condition accounts for hope being a kind of pain, in a similar way as fear. None of them could be good.[15] Moreover, these affects contain a lack of knowledge and an impotence of the mind, and therefore are signs of mental weakness. The free man stands beyond hope and fear.[16] In his attempt to mimic the geometrical method of reasoning, Spinoza says that the greater the fear of an evil, the greater must be the corresponding hope to avoid it, because these affects are proportionate to each other.

The causes for the formation of a political state are hope and fear. The hope for security is primary, since positive thinking is not the exception but the norm. Our nature is to "readily believe what we hope, but hardly believe what we fear, and of both more or less than would be appropriate."[17] People can be governed by these affects, but once hope and fear are gone, man is free.[18]

In the 20th century Gabriel Marcel points out that hope is the cognitive primary affect in man. "Hope may well be the fabric of which our souls are made." He even attributes a metaphysical function to "true hope". He insists that hope is more than just a subjective stimulus. Rather, it is a vital component of any creative process.[19]

Ernst Bloch calls hope the most human of all mental states, a human's basic affect. For him, hope is a "principle" as well as an affection, which intends a forward expansion of the self into some utopia.[20] Bloch sees in everything from matter to man the structure of being in possibility, and being for possibility. Human life is primarily a struggle directed towards the future. The future contains the objects of hope and fear, but naturally mainly what is hoped for. Hope is not passive like fear. False hope is one of the biggest evils of mankind, but true hope is its greatest blessing.[21]

Twentieth century Christianity has further increased the positive evaluation of hope. Jürgen Moltmann defines hope as nothing but the expectation of those things which, according to faith, are truly promised by God.[22] He points out that in medieval time sadness (*tristitia*) was considered a deadly sin, as Johannes Chrysostomos condemns despair, which for many Christian theologians is a sin like doubt and arrogance. Despair is the deliberate refusal to believe that what God promised will be fulfilled. It is a rejection of God's mercy. A consequence of faith is the duty to be happy. This situation also triggers the urge to pretense, and to sometimes just appear happy in order to hide one's unhappiness, the sinful state or remoteness from God.

The hope for victory over evil and death is reflected in prayer for those who suffer and for the dead. The church remains hoping for an eternal life.[23] The late Pope John Paul II said in his book *Crossing the Threshold of Hope*, "God is the first source of joy and hope for man."[24]

Existentialist philosopher Martin Heidegger states that we are thrown into the world, and have a choice of how to make the best of it. The essence of human existence is concern. Hope is not only an affect but a mood. Contrary to former descriptions of hope being the expectation of a future good, Heidegger sees the structure of this phenomenon not just in the future character of the object of hope, but the fact that the act of hoping involves us. In hoping, we imagine ourselves as closer to what we are hoping for. The person who is hoping is ahead of himself.[25]

Albert Camus advocates reason, and prefers clear thought to mere hope; it is better to think more, and hope less. We should not waste our time on God as he is dead. Our fate is death, and hope is no comfort. But the experience of the absurd does not rule out any efforts to make sense. Camus says, "Where there is no hope, it is incumbent on us to invent it."[26]

This selection from the history of philosophy may suffice as a short introduction. We shall now turn to Schopenhauer.

2. Schopenhauer and the Enlightenment

The so-called "enlightenment" was a rational project, while romanticism and pietism could be regarded as a countermovement. Schopenhauer was influenced by both.

The enlightenment usually comprises certain thinkers and a program. In a narrow sense, it also denotes a historical epoch in the 18th century. In a broader sense of its intention, the enlightenment's beginnings can be seen within the natural sciences, linked to the name of Isaac Newton, in the humanities to John Locke, Condillac, Lessing, and in the social sciences to Turgot, Price und Rousseau. In general, reason should provide the foundation for an order of thinking and living, whereby mankind would progress in free necessity towards the true, the good, and happiness on earth. Faith in reason is combined with faith in a wise plan and government of the world, and purpose in history.

Kant defines the term "enlightenment" in an essay of 1784, as man's exit out of his immature intellectual dependency. We have been to blame for our laziness and lack of courage, and Kant tells us to take heart, and use our own brains.[27]

In *Parerga and Paralipomena* Schopenhauer confesses his affinity with Kant's motto of the enlightenment in his chapter on "Thinking for

Oneself" (*Selbstdenken*). Beside Kant, Schopenhauer appreciates most of all the following members of the enlightenment: Voltaire, Rousseau, Sterne, Lichtenberg, Lessing, Schiller and Wieland.[28]

In Schopenhauer's time the motive of the enlightenment was connected with Hegelian thought.[29] It is well known that Schopenhauer and Hegel were opponents with radically different basic principles. In Hegel, the world is the idea in its difference. In Schopenhauer, the world is the self-awareness of the will. Hegel's explanation of the world "out of mind" stands in a long tradition beginning with Anaxagoras, who claims there is an "intellect" (*logos*) and hence an idea or re-presentation, as origin of the real world. Schopenhauer is vehemently opposed to this understanding of enlightenment, which assumes a logical, rational principle of reality, as well as the possibility to thoroughly penetrate and unlock it by means of logical-rational thinking.[30] It is this spirit of en-lightenment within German idealism which Schopenhauer calls "theology."

Does this mean that Schopenhauer is a critic of the enlightenment, instead of a member of the enlightenment? Or is he rather enlightening the enlightenment? Schopenhauer emphasizes in his *Manuscript Remains* that he rejects dishonesty. "We want the truth, and we will vivisect all lies without regret."[31]

Whoever aims at truth unconditionally must not expect that this truth should also be useful, good or beautiful. Knowledge and wisdom can be in conflict with each other. A life-long lie may be pragmatically good without being theoretically true. And among philosophers there are not only critics of ideology, but also ideologists. The meaning of philosophy is love for wisdom. Schopenhauer splits the former unity of the true and the good, since eternal truth is no longer considered by him as being embedded in the good ground of the world. He chooses truth, and the motto in his work *Parerga and Paralipomena* I is: *Vitam impendere vero* [Dedicate one's life to the true] (Juvenal, ›Saturae‹ 4, 91).[32] He insists that it is impossible to serve truth and the world at the same time.

In which areas can we detect elements of the enlightenment in Schopenhauer? We shall use Kant's meaning of enlightenment here, the courage to use one's own faculty of understanding and reasoning in observation of intellectual honesty, and the endeavor to denunciate false ideas.

1. Criticism of purely speculative metaphysics lacking all possible experience;
2. Criticism of religion;
3. Criticism of rationalism concerning the constitution of the world as well as consciousness;
4. Criticism of prejudices and reason corrupted by interests;
6. Criticism of the attempt to teach virtue and the identification of virtue with knowledge;

7. Criticism of language. Many of Kant's followers, according to Schopenhauer, imitated his rather dark writing style to conceal their thoughts or to confuse the readers. The verbose "windbag" Fichte invented this foul method with a purpose to deceive, not to teach. Schopenhauer claims to use common language to express uncommon truths, but they use uncommon words to express commonplaces.[33]

On all of these levels, high hopes play an essential role. In each case they form the implicit foundation on which Schopenhauer casts an eye.

We need to look on Schopenhauer's *relevance* here. Is he still up to date? Towards the end of the 18th century he was very popular. The main reasons may have been high unemployment and shattered hopes for a revolution, and optimistic German idealism becoming less attractive in the overall social misery. Schopenhauer himself denies that his pessimism was largely a result of the cultural climate. He says that it developed between 1814 and 1818, which he calls life's most hopeful time. His philosophy is a reaction to the romantic literature of his time, which was mainly shaped by Goethe's optimism and idea of harmony in the world. Schopenhauer is closer to the moral pessimism of the enlightenment. But he also deviates from Kant and German Idealism.

Schopenhauer was ahead of his time in several offences to man's self-esteem.[34] This was intentional since he writes in a letter to Frauenstädt: "Where is a vanity which I have not offended?"[35] These offences are:

1) The cosmological offence. Earth is merely one of countless spheres in the universe covered with a moldy film of living and knowing beings;[36]

2) The biological offence. Man and animals are essentially the same, as they share the same will-to-live. Man's greater intellect is mainly the will's tool and servant compensating his lack of instincts. "If we descend through the series of grades of animals, we see the intellect becoming weaker and weaker and more and more imperfect; but we certainly do not observe a corresponding degradation of the will."[37]

3) The psychological offence. The ego is not the master in our consciousness.[38]

The central idea of the enlightenment, thinking for oneself, is appealing at all times. Critical thinking is a never ending effort. As in modern science, every philosophical insight always needs to be defended against newly emerging mystifications. Schopenhauer's position does not offer consolation or convey a happy message. This tends to make it hard to accept for most people. The majority is not attracted to a philosophy of disenchantment, because the will to live wants to be flattered. Theology and optimism meet this demand. *Mundus vult decipi* – the world wants to be deceived. And those who shed light on these negative aspects often get ignored or silenced. Schopenhauer can still serve as an educator in our time, because he worships no idols[39] and attacks illusions in a way from which we can learn.

2.1 Criticism of Ideology

The term "ideology" can be traced back to the French thinker Destutt de Tracy (1754-1836) who follows Locke and Condillac. It means the elucidation of the origins of ideas and structural foundations of state, society, church and other institutions. In this sense it is an investigation of ideas.

After Napoleon the term's meaning changes, and from that time until today denotes maladaptive rules, theories and programs which involve deceptive motives. To summarize, ideology is an interpretative scheme guided – often unconsciously - by interests. It may be introduced on purpose, to manipulate people in certain directions, and is likely to create "false consciousness" among its recipients. In this sense it can be regarded as a formation of an irrational belief system by means of apparently rational arguments, and deception of the mind. Man errs because he is satisfied by judgments without sufficient reason. If he fails to wake up from his "dogmatic slumber" (Kant) and thus remains intellectually immature, it is his own fault. But enlightenment is the way out. Critique of ideology aims to explain the fact of illusions, various handicaps of reasoning and flaws in thinking. It pertains not only to overt lies but also to the covert persuaders of human reason.[40]

The struggle against ideology has a long tradition. Francis Bacon deals in his *Novum Organon*

(1620) with idols of the soul which prevent truth from entering. Helvétius and Holbach are dedicated to unmasking prejudices. They see irrational repression in politics. Thomas Hobbes mentions the roles of hope and fear to manipulate people in this main work *Leviathan* and Spinoza picks up on this thought.

Karl Marx (1818-1883) is regarded as the classical critic of ideology. Both Marx and Schopenhauer want to turn Hegel upside down. They deny the primacy of reason. But Marx still had hope. He did not believe that man's consciousness determined his life, but on the contrary that his social environment determined his consciousness. In his opinion all that was needed was a change of the material situation to correct this false consciousness.

Schopenhauer disagrees with both Hegel and Marx. Each individual has to start at point zero. Everybody gets immersed in ideas produced by others before he can begin to use his own reason. Therefore enlightenment cannot only go on and on, but has to be starting anew all the time. And there must always be a distinction made between a critique of ideology, and an ideological critique. Namely, a critique is not immune to mystification either, and critical works have premises which have to be questioned, too. As diagnosed by Max Horkheimer and Theodor Adorno in the *Dialectic of Enlightenment* (1944), criticism has a tendency to turn into theory, and theory to turn into jargon.

Some explanations which are satisfactory at a given time, may lose their explanatory and enlightening power over time because of changes in reality, and then they may become ideological theories themselves. If they are not questioned and put to the test, they prevent a fresh start to find a better explanation.

Schopenhauer attempts to demonstrate the origins and conditions of our thinking, and include them in his critique of reason. The intellect is created by the will to live in order to serve the organism in its quest for survival. It is the will's tool. The intellect's shortcomings are due to the fact that it is an instrument of the will to live. It emerged out of it and is usually merely its servant. And man is no longer considered as radically different from animals. They share the same will to live, and the "human intellect is only a higher degree of the animal intellect".[41] This view is already a forerunner of a bio-philosophical episte-mology.

The aim of Schopenhauer's theory of knowledge is to reveal the hidden influences on thought. They can be found in the struggle for survival, sexuality, all sorts of needs, and striving for pleasure and power. These are the true masters and they are far from being reasonable. They precede all practical and applied reason. This authentic, true background - the instincts and interests - permeates all areas of life below the surface. They lurk behind the big words of religious, political and social institutions and ideologies. Such training does not spring from common sense nor our own judgment. Especially children are vaccinated with such prejudices and, according to Schopenhauer, the dismantling of early acquired indoctrinations takes up the largest part of our lives.

> Man even surpasses all the lower order of animals in his capacity for being trained. [...] There is no absurdity, however palpable it may be, which may not be fixed in the minds of all men, if it is inculcated before they are six years old by continual and earnest repetition.[42]

Education has the task to painfully deconstruct such blindly imitated beliefs and habits again.

For Schopenhauer history is devoid of reason, as there are just some variations of the same theme. It is basically always the same, but slightly different: "*eadem, sed aliter*". It is the expression of the blind will which moves individuals as well as crowds. While originally and in itself blind, the will is illuminated by the intellect. But the intellect is most often guided by ideas or ideologies. The intellect is naturally equipped with a bias towards its advantage and profit. In my opinion Schopenhauer's main relevance lies in his approach to a critique of ideology.

2.2 The Irrational

The so-called "irrational" is a term not used by Schopenhauer himself. Wilhelm Windelband was the first to ascribe irrationalism to Schopenhauer in his *History of Modern Philosophy* in 1880,[43] followed by Heinrich Hasse (1908; 1913) and others. The label "irrational" culminated in the vehement accusation of being a "destroyer of reason" by Georg Lukács in 1952.

This label was motivated in the fact that for Schopenhauer the world is not rooted in reason. And he thinks less of concepts and reasoning than is typical for the rational tradition. Instead, he appreciates intuitive knowledge and considers experience and perception as valuable teachers.

The rational tradition can be traced as far back as the world principle of reason (*nous*) in Anaxagoras. Schopenhauer's predecessor and much admired Kant was the first to open the door to irrationalism. According to his transcendental philosophy all possible experience appears under the subjective forms of knowledge. These are time and space as forms of intuition and the concepts *a priori*, mainly causality. Every known thing presupposes the underlying thing-in-itself. And these things as they are in themselves, independent of subjective forms of knowledge, are the challenge.

Philosophy begins with marvel. Schopenhauer doubts revelation and refuses to deduce the world from dogma. Mere hearsay or speculative meta-physics are not fit to provide certain knowledge. We can only know something which is an object or form of possible experience. However, all experience is based on something inexplicable. This foundation cannot be completely fathomed by empirical science, but it is presupposed. No rational ground can be assigned to the "forces of nature and the definite mode of operation of things, the quality or character of every phenomenon […]."[44] While a cause can be given for every single effect, no cause can be found for a thing's specific mode of operation, it remains an occult quality. Therefore not only science stays locked out, but also philosophy. Both face that last inexplicable element, the rest which is left by the irrational connection of any two items. Forever inexplicable, therefore, remain 1) the course of time, 2) the laws of spatial position, 3) the relationship between cause and effect, 4) the relationship of a judgment to the reason which makes it true, 5) the force of a motive.[45]

The principle of all explanation is the principle of sufficient reason. And all knowledge, by working in accordance with this principle, reaches a border. Just as in its particular manifestations, the world as a whole remains a total mystery. It resists all justification. It is not possible to render a reason or cause of its being, nor demonstrate that it exists to its own advantage.

Although Schopenhauer insists on the inexplicable, he opens a loophole for insight. He claims that each of us can become aware of the ultimate reality immediately in self-consciousness. Even though it does not appear fully as it is in itself, at least it appears at its closest to it. We are aware of our body not only as a representation of an object among others, but also as our will-to-live. Our own well-being is our utmost interest, and any harm is immediately perceived either as physical and/or mental pain. We become aware of ourselves as will. At least a partial recognizability of the will must be assumed. If this were not so, we would not be able to talk about it at all. But what man learns to know here is nothing like knowledge. On its lower stages of objectification the will lacks all consciousness. The intellect with its faculty of concept formation and reasoning emerges only late in the hierarchy of life in animal organisms. Stripped of all subjective forms of knowledge, the will is outside of time and space as well as beyond causality.

Schopenhauer's philosophy is essentially an elaboration on the "mystery as such", the explanation of the unity of the knowing and the willing subject. The fact of this unity cannot be rationally argued nor grasped. Hence the term "explanation" does not mean giving a reason or cause for a consequence here, but something like an interpretation. Schopenhauer says that the aim of his philosophy is the elucidation of the connection between the appearance and its essence. Knowledge is forced to acknowledge something "irrational" by reaching a limit which is totally different from itself. It is not an idea but will. This evident reality is not just represented in the mind, but it is what we *are*. The irrational is not known as such, but it is the irrational which becomes conscious of itself under the forms of rationality.

Schopenhauer waives a "proof for the reality of the outer world" as Kant provides in the second edition of the *Critique of Pure Reason*. Instead, he relies on common sense and then infers, by analogy from one's own felt reality, to the reality of other appearances. He further states that not only must man be understood out of nature, but also nature out of man. Schopenhauer opposes the primacy of the rational principle. Reality in itself is not just a subjective condition of the possibility of nature. In the beginning there is not "the word" (*logos*) and no intelligence, no plan. "The world has not been created by an intellect, but it is rather the other way round: the world has created the intellect." The intellect is nature's product. Its last one, the highest, though it just came into being randomly, but could also have not emerged, as it is indeed most often absent. The unconscious struggle to survive, though, is always present. This irrational desire does not stem from reason, since then it would never have agreed to such an unprofitable "business" as life. Life is finite and miserable. Schopenhauer concludes that the will to live is "dumb." This view makes him a thinker against the stream at his time which was dominated by the rationalism of German idealism.

The groundlessness of the endless striving of man for happiness and his constant suffering is regarded as analogous to the endless expansion of the universe where the world principle is at work. As long as our mind is filled with our desire, as long as we are subjected to our wishes, along with hopes and fears, as long as we are subjects of the will, we shall never obtain lasting happiness, or peace. The strife for happiness is a constant torture, and can never be really satisfied. While each individual wish has a cause, desire as such has no cause or reason. The blind will to live does not result from any preceding insight into the worth of life. We do not want to live because life is so attractive. Being is futile and everything that exists must vanish. But this fact does not change our unconditional adherence to life. Schopenhauer draws our attention to the fact that nature wastes so much in the proliferation of germs, the ease and large numbers with which life comes into being. To this it makes a ridiculous contrast to consider the unbelievable tumult of an individual who faces death. As if it were of the highest importance to stay a little longer away from where sooner or later he will be forever – or not be, as a matter of fact. How unreasonable.

Logic, as the system of the rules of right thinking, is degraded by Schopenhauer to the rank of a tool, in opposition to Hegel. Concepts are inevitably insufficient, though necessary. If they are formed properly, they are produced by abstraction from perception, which is why they are emptier and poorer than the original.[46] Concepts are foreign to the will, while *music* is a more immediate expression of it. However, philosophy relies on clear and distinct concepts. It must use reasonable discourse to be communicable. While Schopenhauer's object of philosophy is irrational, his method remains fully rational. Schopenhauer does not give up on rational knowledge and language, nor does he deify the irrational. On the contrary, he treats it as something to be overcome.

I. Ethics of Communication

The restriction of hope to probability pertains not only to behavior affecting one's own desires (which is discussed below within a theory of happiness as an ethics of belief).

Hope also involves an interactive ethical component. The creation or nourishment of false hopes in others violates rules of ethical communication. Speaking the truth and keeping one's promises involve the duty not to disappoint others. Others may hope that a person who makes a promise will keep his word, which is a fundamental basis of trust in a community.

An action has moral value for Schopenhauer if its motive is another individual's well-being. Since another's woe is felt less intensely than one's own, and pain is felt more strongly than happiness, it is the identification with another being which brings about compassion as the source of all true, unselfish virtue.

In his work *On the Basis of Morality* Schopenhauer counts justice and love as cardinal virtues, according to their degrees of compassion. From the first degree of compassion springs the maxim, "Do harm to no one" (*neminem laede*), which is the principle of justice. From the second degree flows *caritas*, pure philanthropy along with the urge to help as much as possible (*omnes, quantum potes, iuva*).[47] This attitude is also extended to animals, even to plants and the whole of nature, and then becomes a general loving-kindness towards all beings.

> If my nature is susceptible of Compassion up to this point, then it will avail to keep me back, whenever I should like to use others' pain as a means to obtain my ends; equally, whether this pain be immediate, or an after-consequence, whether it be effected directly, or indirectly, through intermediate links. I shall therefore lay hands on the property as little as on the person of another, and avoid causing him distress, no less mental than bodily. I shall thus not only abstain from doing him physical injury, but also, with equal care I shall guard against inflicting on him the suffering of mind, which mortification and calumny, anxiety and vexation so surely work.[48]

Injustice can be done by either violence or a trick. The malice consists in presenting, to the other person's intellect, wrong motives intended to deceive him, and cause him to act to the trickster's advantage. This is done by means of lies. The injustice of false pretense lies in being a tool of malice. It presents lies to force actions through wrong motivations, in an attempt to control others.

Causing wrong expectations and unjustified hopes involves not only an attempt to manipulate others according to one's own interest, but their later disappointment is programmed as well. Those who nourish false hopes light-heartedly, which are not later met, participate in the other's pain and are to blame for it. This is why promises and contracts are morally binding. If they are breached, they turn out to be despicable lies.

In some cases though, compassion may also lead to the withholding of an unpleasant truth or a white lie. Perhaps I would not want to take away somebody's hope, seeing how much he clings to it, and that this hope has a beneficial function for him. Contrary to Kant, Schopenhauer allows for a right to lie out of sympathy.

II. Ethics of Belief

Deception of others has just been discussed within an ethics of communication, while self-deception belongs to an ethics of belief. Humans are more prone to error and falsehood than animals: man is a liar through and through, cheating both himself and others. These masks, illusions and errors result from the influence of the will on the intellect. Schopenhauer thinks that logic is practically useless since *wrong conclusions* are very rare. But *wrong judgments* are most common, and logic does not help at all to correct them.

But "what means all will to truth?" Nietzsche asks. The truth makes free of error. Knowledge is an advantage. Knowledge is power. Maybe the truth makes one happy, too. Happiness does not rest on the intensity of the positive emotion, but on its duration. Schopenhauer agrees with Aristotle's statement in the *Nicomachean Ethics*: "One swallow does not make a summer, nor does one day; and so too one day, or a short time, does not make a man blessed and happy." (Book I, 1098.a18).[49]

Every intense joy is mixed with bitterness because it is transient, and bonds man on the wheel of fortune. Fortune is futile and can change any moment. Once out of luck, loss is suffered and grief results. Unfulfilled hope is followed by the affect of disappointment. Shattered hope hits with violence. The greater the preceding hope was, the

45

greater is the negative affect of sadness or anger and the feeling of emptiness. The term "disappointment" suggests the absence of an expected appointment. Hope contains the possibility of error, because it is directed towards an uncertain future. Hope implies an inadequate idea, because it assumes something as true which later turns out to be false. This inadequate idea accounts for the risk factor in hoping. A life of hope is a life of risk. But perhaps only a life with risk is real life, and who does not hope anymore, does not really live anymore.

Animals are less bothered by the unpleasant concern for their maintenance and the uncertainties of hope. But maybe their lives are therefore poorer in joy since hope anticipates a happier future. This vivid imagination is the source of man's greatest joy and pleasure, which animals lack. They could therefore be called "hopeless." However, it is just this trait, the fact that they live in the moment, which makes animals display greater calmness and serenity.

> The chief source of all this passion is that thought for what is absent and future, which, with man, exercises such a powerful influence upon all he does. It is this that is the real origin of his cares, his hopes, his fears - emotions which affect him much more deeply than could ever be the case with those present joys and sufferings to which the brute is confined. [50]

But man does not get "the joys of hope and anticipation" for free. Namely, what somebody enjoys through hope and expectation is later deducted from the real event, as it turns out less satisfactorily than expected.

Hope is also a consolation. The comfort it provides may be self-deception or an illusion. The affect of hope, similar to that of fear, gives a blurred vision.

> How little absolute sincerity is to be expected, even from persons otherwise honest, whenever their interest in any way bears on a matter, can be judged from the fact that we so often deceive ourselves where hope bribes us, or fear befools us [...].[51]

The loss of hope can lead to despair in man. Hopelessness is forced upon him and is an unnatural condition.

> He who has given up hope has also given up fear; this is the meaning of the expression *desperate*. It is natural for a man to have faith in what he wishes, and to have faith in it because he wishes it. If this peculiarity of his nature, which is both beneficial and comforting, is eradicated by repeated hard blows of fate, and he is brought to a converse condition, when he believes that something must happen because he does not wish it, and what he wishes can never happen just because he wishes it; this is, in reality, the state which has been called *desperation*.[52]

Despair can create a subjective hell if somebody clearly recognizes the aim of his willing and also realizes that he can never reach it, but nevertheless keeps willing it. Schopenhauer also stresses in his *Manuscript Remains* that if man cannot stop willing, and there is no hope to ever be satisfied, the will becomes a terrible torture.[53] If the object of desire is so unreachable that there is no hope left to ever attain it, then despair enters.

Insight into this mechanism makes one wonder whether it could be possible to overcome hope, or to voluntarily choose resignation in order to prevent future pain, and so become invulnerable. Such an attempt would be different from hopelessness or despair. The difference is that in the former case, the will is quiet. In the latter case, the will is not negated and keeps willing desperately. Schopenhauer quotes Horace (*Epist.* I, xviii, 97), who gives advice how to take it easy, and live your life without being tormented by endless desire, fear and hope for things of little use.[54]

The aim of Stoic ethics was a happy life. They had also learned from experience that "every wish soon dies and so can beget no more pain, if no hope nourishes it."[55] Happiness depends on the proportion of what we desire and what we receive.[56]

We usually feel joy much weaker than expected, but pain much greater than expected.[57] Pain only is felt intensely. As the greed for life is endless and insatiable, therefore never to be fulfilled and no lasting happiness attainable, redemption can only be conceived as the mortification of the will.[58] Asceticism is the deliberate breaking of the will-to-live to reach peace of mind. Knowledge of the futile nature of everything and the ways of the world become the quieter of the will. The will either turns around against itself or stops willing. It is not exactly clear what Schopenhauer means here, but it would be more plausible to consider it an unwilling, or the absence of willing so that only the pure subject of knowledge remains in consciousness. This is very difficult to achieve though and even more difficult to make it last.

> The allurements of hope, the flattery of the present, the sweetness of pleasures, the well-being that falls to the lot of our person amid the lamentations of a suffering world governed by chance and error, all these draw us back to it, and rivet the bonds anew.[59]

Schopenhauer disagrees with the Stoics because they believe in happiness, while he thinks that happiness is impossible. As for Buddha, for Schopenhauer all life is suffering,[60] which the pursuit of happiness only increases. It is a contradiction to wish to live completely without pain and grief. Individuals are finite beings who are always threatened by stronger forces, and they necessarily become diminished and annihilated in the end. The wise man does not pursue happiness, but tries to avoid great unhappiness as far as possible. In his *Manuscript Remains*, Schopenhauer tells us that if we do not want to become very unhappy, a sure way is not to ask to become very happy. This is wise advice because it is very easy to be very unhappy, while to be very happy is not only difficult but totally impossible.[61] Since happiness depends on a mathematical proportion between what is desired and what is attained, it can be manipulated by either working on the first number or on the second, but only the wise man chooses to cut down on his desires.

It may sound strange that Schopenhauer even assigns a positive role, not only to asceticism but also to blows of fate. He says that fate has an important effect on our contentment or discontent. A sudden great mischief, which throws us far back and crushes quite many of our wishes, works as well, for our peace of mind, as does some good fortune which gives us more than we had been hoping for, which then gives birth to many more hopes to trouble us afterwards.[62]

Looking at the world and mankind, Schopenhauer concludes that there is misery everywhere. Life is characterized by daily struggles, concerns and worries, fights and wars. And the fear and anguish of a single troubled individual causes an imbalance and disharmony which makes it impossible to justify the world. Despite all improvements of civilization, the demands and problems and pains persist. The woes of social restriction and conflict, competition, toil, boredom, disease and death remain. So do the pains of failure, envy, jealousy, unfulfilled desires and unsatisfied hopes.

II.1. The Bribed Reason

Schopenhauer makes a turn in ontology. He states that the world was not made by an intellect, but that the world made the intellect. The world is the precondition of the intellect. Nature is what causes, drives and creates without mediation of an intellect. Since the world made itself without any help from knowledge, its essence cannot be fully grasped by knowledge, and all knowledge presupposes the world already.

What presupposes the world, however, lies beyond our forms of knowledge and therefore is assumed by Schopenhauer to be inexplicable, groundless. We can approach it, though, through the experience of our own self as a willing being.

Schopenhauer draws a clear dividing line between will and intellect. They are fundamentally different, but can interact. The relationship between the two, however, is such that the will dominates the intellect, like its master. In Psychology, Schopenhauer establishes a so-called Copernican turn after an earlier model. Nicolaus Copernicus formulated a heliocentric model in the Renaissance. He claimed that it is not the sun which revolves around the earth, but that the earth revolves around the sun. Kant applied this idea of a turn to his theory of knowledge and claimed that experience is constituted by subjective conditions.

Schopenhauer uses a turn, too. He turns around the master and servant relationship in the mind. Unlike in the past, where the intellect was thought to reign, it now becomes the will to live. From this can be concluded that the will corrupts almost every step of the intellect.

> Indeed, many may have made the observation that, if a matter of importance to them admits of several courses of development, and they have brought all these into one disjunctive judgment that in their opinion is complete, the outcome is nevertheless quite different and wholly unexpected by them. But possibly they will not have noticed that this result was then almost always the one most unfavorable to them. This can be explained from the fact that, while their *intellect* imagined that it surveyed the possibilities completely, the worst of all remained quite invisible to it, because the *will*, so to speak, kept this covered with its hand; in other words, the will so mastered the intellect that it was quite incapable of glancing at the worst case of all, although, this case was the most probable, since it actually came to pass. [63]

As soon as the first few data are collected about a given situation, the always ready and never tired will pops up from the depths of the soul and shows up as shock, fear, hope, joy, desire, envy, grief, ambition, anger, rage etc. and drives one to rash words or deeds, which are usually followed by remorse. Interest seduces one to make hasty judgments, before the intellect has finished its reflections.

Schopenhauer's criticism of the "bribed reason" has a long tradition. We should mention Francis Bacon and his theory of idols as well as René Descartes and Baruch Spinoza in the 17th century with their aim to deconstruct the prejudices, and finally Immanuel Kant and his critique of reason in order to determine its limits. The question of how far the competence of reason goes is the main theme in an ideological conflict.

For Schopenhauer reason is corrupted, namely bribed by interest in one's own advantage. "Thus is our intellect daily befooled and corrupted by the deceptions of inclination and liking."[64] Emotions and affections are reactions to this kind of satisfaction or dissatisfaction of the will, and falsify our judgments.

> Our *advantage*, of whatever kind it may be, exercises a similar secret power over our judgment; what is in agreement with it at once seems to us fair, just, and reasonable. What runs counter to it is presented to us in all seriousness as unjust and outrageous, or inexpedient and absurd. Hence so many prejudices of social position, rank, profession, nationality, sect, and religion. A hypothesis, conceived and formed, makes us lynx-eyed for everything that confirms it, and blind to everything that contradicts it.[65]

Despite their differences, Schopenhauer agrees with Descartes insofar as for him also, faulty judgments are caused by extensive and unrestricted use of the faculty of affirmation or "will". Errors happen when belief kicks in too early without clear and distinct comprehension. There is a will to believe, especially with regard to hope. The intellect's calculation of the probability is overrun by an act of will.

> These inner and essential imperfections of the intellect are further increased by […]the influence that the *will* exerts on all its operations, as soon as that will is in any way concerned in their result. Every passion, in fact every inclination or disinclination, tinges the objects of knowledge with its color. Most common occurrence is the falsification of knowledge brought about by desire and hope, since they show us the scarcely possible in dazzling colors as probable and well-nigh certain, and render us almost incapable of comprehending what is opposed to it.[66]

To break free from such illusions, the faculty of judgment has to be disciplined. The will to believe has to be suppressed and kept within the limits of the understanding. This requires a strong mind and a lot of self-discipline. "What opposes the heart is not admitted by the head." Schopenhauer thinks that most people prefer to enjoy the pleasures of illusions to the truth. Only a few have a will to know which is strong enough to take pains to gain intellectual maturity. Some scholars have therefore accused Schopenhauer of elitism in epistemology. But to part with prejudices is just not for everyone.

On its higher stages, the will-to-live has created a lantern, the intellect. The intellect has severe shortcomings though. For example, it relies on perception and concepts which reduce the manifold. Given its natural origin, it is primarily a tool in the struggle for survival. The interests of life influence its performance in many ways. It is extremely difficult to get a clear picture of anything in which we are interested. It is hardly possible, since the will immediately interferes with every argument and every added data. The voice of the will cannot easily be distinguished from the voice of the intellect, because both are merged into *one*, the ego. This is manifested especially whenever we want to make a guess on the outcome of something. Here interest falsifies almost every move of the intellect, be it as fear, be it as hope. It is hardly possible to see clearly, because the intellect resembles a torch for reading which is flickering in a strong breeze.[67]

Nevertheless the intellect does have room for objective insight, even for philosophical truth. The more the willing disappears from consciousness, the more subjective distortion is filtered out. And the more individuality vanishes, the less sorrow and pain are felt.

> As will, and therefore as individual, he is only one, and that one exclusively, which gives him plenty to do and to suffer. As that which makes a purely objective representation he is the pure subject of

knowledge, and only in the consciousness of this does the objective world have its existence. As such he is *all things*, in so far as he perceives them, and in him their existence is without burden and hardship.[68]

II.2. The "Folly of the Heart"

When the intellect's probability calculus is disturbed by wishful thinking, hope results.

> *Hope* is to confuse the desire that something should occur with the probability that it will. Perhaps no man is free from this folly of the heart, which deranges the intellect's correct estimation of probability to such a degree as to make him think the event quite possible, even if the chances are only a thousand to one. And still, an unexpected misfortune is like a speedy death-stroke; while a hope that is always frustrated, and yet springs into life again, is like death by slow torture.[69]

The unwarranted anticipation of satisfaction comes directly from the influence of willing in the representation. Not only are the real perspectives weighed, but the objectively unlikely scenario is believed to be probable. Desire anticipates the wanted object or event and represents the future joy, but without actually feeling it because it is blended with painful doubt and uncertainty. The present involves the feeling of something lacking which is not yet achieved, and this inflicts some discomfort.

Hope is wishful thinking and as such, one-sided. The origin of hope out of desire leads to a wrong assessment of the situation, and can even make one mentally blind.

> What is opposed to our part, our plan, our wish, or our hope often cannot possibly be grasped and comprehended by us, whereas it is clear to the eyes of everyone else; on the other hand, what is favorable to these leaps to our eyes from afar. What opposes the heart is not admitted by the head.[70]

The imperfections of the intellect are much increased by the disturbances of the will. Every passion as well as every like or dislike tinges the objects of knowledge and blurs the image so that the eye cannot function as "clear mirror of the world".

> But this disturbing influence of the will's activity on the intellect can be shown not only in the perturbations produced by the emotions, but also in many other more gradual, and therefore more lasting, falsifications of thought through our inclinations and tendencies. *Hope* makes us regard what we desire, and *fear* what we are afraid of, as being probable and near, and both magnify their object. [...] Its nature lies in the fact that the will, when its servant, the *intellect*, is unable to produce the thing desired, compels this servant at any rate to picture this thing to it, and generally to undertake the role of comforter, to pacify its lord and master, as a nurse does a child, with fairy-tales, and to deck these out so that they obtain an appearance of verisimilitude.[71]

For all intellectual endeavors, it holds true that interest always leads to merely mediocre, pragmatic insights. It is just this trait which characterizes the average human being, the "run-of-the-mill product of nature." To be a genius, it would be necessary to be free from the passions. The most perfect knowledge is the purely objective apprehension of the world, which relies on the silence of the will.

However, it is not always the case that the activity of the will has a purely negative impact on thinking. Schopenhauer quotes Bacon's metaphor, that the intellect is a light which receives oil to burn from the will and the passions.[72] Memory and performance can be enhanced by interest. The spur of the will can work as an incentive. It may support the intellect. It also heightens the emotions and even makes passions possible which animals do not have in the same manner. "The vehemence of the will keeps pace with the enhancement of intelligence."[73]

> A powerfully acting motive, such as yearning desire or pressing need, sometimes raises the intellect to a degree of which we had never previously believed it capable. [...] The understanding of the stupidest person becomes keen when it is a question of objects that closely concern his willing. He now observes, notices, and distinguishes with great subtlety and refinement even the smallest circumstances that have reference to his desires or fears.[74]

Positive anticipation often functions as incentive for action. This is why hope is often considered indispensable for any success.

It is not always necessary to have a clear idea or anticipation of what is being hoped for. Hope can be unspecific. Hoping for a miracle may be lifesaving. The following fable was originally written by the Greek poet Aesop around 550 BC. A frog whose pond had dried out was hopping around a farmyard. In the barn he discovered a pail half-filled with fresh milk and when looking in he slipped and fell in. Since the sides of the pail were too steep and the bottom too deep he could not get out again. For many hours he was frantically kicking and squirming getting very exhausted, until at last the milk had turned into a solid hunk of butter and he could jump out of the pail.

Line art illustration of frog public domain image.[75]

This anecdote has a different version featuring two frogs in the same situation. One of them gave up hope, stopped kicking, and drowned. The other frog did not give up hope of surviving, even in an apparently hopeless situation, and was saved because of his struggles, to his own surprise.

Although Schopenhauer is mainly a philosopher of resignation, he is also a philosopher of resistance, even of a cosmic revolt. In his *Aphorisms* on wisdom he emphasizes that even when the outcome of a dangerous situation is doubtful, we must not give up, but should resist for as long as there is the slightest possibility that it might work out all right.[76]

II.3. The Passion of Hope

Schopenhauer has not developed a systematic theory of the affections, but relies much on past teachings. At times his account sounds pretty much in line with both Descartes and Spinoza.

> *Passion* is an inclination so strong, that the motives that excite it exercise a power over the will which is stronger than that of any possible motive acting against them. Its mastery over the will thus becomes absolute; consequently, the attitude of the will towards it is *passive*, an attitude of *suffering*. [...] The *emotion* is a stirring of the will, just as irresistible [as a passion] yet only temporary, by a motive that does not obtain its power through a deep-rooted inclination.[77]

Schopenhauer employs a meaning of "will" here which at first sight resembles the use of the term by the rationalist thinkers. Both Descartes and Spinoza identify the will with the faculty of affirmation in a judgment. For them the will is a spontaneous act of mind. It is an intentional decision and works as the antagonist of the affections trying to control them. We are all familiar with situations when our desires are in conflict with each other. This is when we speak of will-power in connection with battling vices, for example. Moreover, not all of our desires are in our best interest, and we may choose an option according to our insight or our drive. Unlike Descartes, though, Schopenhauer denies free will.

We cannot choose who we want to be. Rather, the motive which makes the strongest impression on our character wins. Moreover, he criticizes both Descartes and Spinoza for identifying the will with the faculty of judgment. He stresses that the will as a kind of blindly striving force, is radically different from insight, and even from consciousness. However, a similar striving as the basis for all passions was already assumed by Augustine and the rationalists. As a matter of fact, Schopenhauer has far more in common with Spinoza on this point than he is aware of, or admits. Spinoza introduces such a principle also, which he calls the striving for self-preservation (*conatus in suo esse perseverandi*). This is the kernel of all things, animate or inanimate, and the matrix of all affects. Schopenhauer's principle of the universal will-to-live can be regarded as a functional equivalent.[78] The difference is mainly just a matter of terminology, where Schopenhauer's use of the word "will" is slightly misleading.

> Every *emotion* (*animi perturbatio*) arises simply from the fact that a representation acting on our will comes so extremely near to us that it conceals from us everything else, and we are no longer able to see anything but it.[79]

Since the emotion is an irresistible, temporary stirring of the will by a motive, it takes away intellectual freedom, because not all motives can be contemplated in the same manner. Rational judgment is overrun and rendered "passive", being swept away like in a tsunami.

In his "Psychological Observations" Schopenhauer discusses several affections such as fear, anger, grief, remorse, concern, happiness and unhappiness, despair, hope and others.

The emotions are vehicles of truth, because only in their outbursts does the will to live show up without disguise. We believe people who are upset. In "outbursts of affection and passion the will exhibits itself unveiled. This is precisely why passion, when it speaks, always carries conviction, whatever the passion may be; and rightly so."[80]

But the affections also strip one's individuality and leave merely the generic character, that which is ordinary, and even vulgar. The will to live is what everything is in itself, regardless of subjective forms of knowledge, and hence also lies beyond space and time, the principle of individuation. The will therefore is assumed as one. It is what all beings share. We have it in common with all people, and all animals, even further down to all things in nature. In this, we are all equal and regular. Every outburst of the will to live degrades us to a mere sample of the species because it is the character of the species we are showing at that moment, not our individuality or what makes us special and unique.[81]

The conflict between impulse and thought is a constant challenge for man. He has a choice between giving in to temptation or self-control, spontaneity or deliberation. In order to cope with life and get along in the world, a certain proportion of will and intellect is needed. Since the will moves and the intellect sees, so to speak, it would be necessary for a person with great emotions to also have a great intellect. Every disharmony between the will and the intellect tends to make a person unhappy.[82]

The emotions are also vehicles of illusions. They lead to faulty thinking because they obstruct clear sight and thought. They glare, and make us biased. We see only what we want to see, and nothing else. Objects appear differently from what they are, or how we would apprehend them in a different state of mind. The strength of impressions depends on the strength of emotional arousal.

Every event which causes an unpleasant emotion will leave a lasting effect in our mind, even if it is trifling. As long as it lingers it will obstruct the clear, objective grasp of things and circumstances. It will even tinge all of our thoughts, like a tiny object brought close to our eye distorts our vision.[83]

A special role is played by closeness in time, in affectively loaded reactions. Emotions rely on the present moment, during which they mainly exist just like the will. This intensity fades over time. Small objects in space appear big when close, but turn small and insignificant when further away. It is similar with objects in time. The events and accidents taking place in our daily lives appear important to us as long as they are present or close in time. They cause us all sorts of emotions. But as soon as the flux of time has moved them further away, they become insignificant, not worthy of any attention and soon forgotten, because their apparent size was based on nothing but their proximity.[84]

Affections are all stirrings of the will, while *emotions* are momentary reactions, and *passions* last longer. Passions also lack certainty of knowledge, and distort the objective apprehension of reality. *Hope* is usually ranked among the passions because it often involves something like an attitude which makes hope more persistent than a fleeting emotion.

> But this disturbing influence of the will's activity on the intellect can be shown not only in the perturbations produced by the emotions, but also in many other more gradual, and therefore more lasting, falsifications of thought through our inclinations and tendencies. *Hope* makes us regard what we desire, and *fear* what we are afraid of, as being probable and near, and both magnify their object.[85]

II.4. A "Wicked Way of Thinking"

According to Schopenhauer, hope is based on faith. It can manifest itself not only as a passing arousal, but also as a durable attitude, or even world view (*Weltanschauung*). Therefore it can be treated within the larger framework of optimism.

Contemporary common sense defines an optimist as somebody who rather expects the good than the bad. It is somebody for whom a glass of water is half full instead of half empty as it appears to the pessimist. The pessimist says, "All women are bad", and the optimist replies, "I hope so."

The original meaning of optimism is different, though. The concept of optimism can be traced back to Leibniz who argues in his *Theodicy* that "this world is the best of all possible worlds" (*mundus optimus*). Optimism as a world view is derived from theology. For optimism the world – and God – is justified. In *Genesis* we read after each completed act of creation, "and God saw that it was good." Schopenhauer criticizes this idea of a God who is applauding himself.

> But that a God like Jehovah should have created this world of misery and woe, out of pure caprice, and because he enjoyed doing it, and should then have clapped his hands in praise of his own work, and declared everything to be very good — that will not do at all![86]

But if the Bible is considered as God's word and absolute truth beyond doubt, there is nothing bad about it, and it is blasphemy to point one's finger at it. Then man's task is to dance and be happy. The optimistic theology implies a duty to be happy. Sadness (*tristitia*) was considered a sin in medieval times. Later Kierkegaard observes in this philosophical writing on theology (1849) that "the sickness unto death" is "despair". By "death" he means the loss of eternal life due to sin. Somebody who accepts God's offer for salvation has to be happy, not desperate.

Besides being socially sanctioned and religiously expected, optimism is also the natural and original impulse of any man who has not been broken by too many disasters. Therefore every encouragement and advice not to give up hope generally meets open ears, while it really is just an echo of one's own inner condition. It is natural for everybody to easily believe what he wishes, and to believe it because he wishes it.

Schopenhauer observes that people, who are suddenly notified of a good fortune, easily get killed by such a message, but not by an announcement about a misfortune. He explains this strange fact in his "Psychological Observations" as follows:

> This is why, as is well known, one is so careful to get a man first to hope for happiness before announcing it, then to suggest the prospect of it, then little by little make it known, until gradually all

is known to him; every portion of the revelation loses the strength of its effect because it is anticipated by a demand, and room is still left for more. In virtue of all this, it might be said that our stomach for good fortune is bottomless, but the entrance to it is narrow. What has been said does not apply to sudden misfortunes in the same way. Since hope always resists them, they are for this reason rarely fatal. That fear does not perform an analogous office in cases of good fortune is due to the fact that we are instinctively more inclined to hope than to fear; just as our eyes turn of themselves to light in preference to darkness.[87]

However, optimism is more typical and frequent in youth. Later in life modesty and worries dominate, caused by the many disappointments and bad experiences. During the first half of life we are longing for happiness, during the second half we are trying to avoid unhappiness.[88] Happiness, according to Schopenhauer, is only felt as a release from a preceding need. Well-being is not even a positive entity like its opposite, pain and want.

Not only do the different stages in life make a difference in susceptibility for optimism. Temper also is a factor. The realist is sober, while the optimist is enthusiastic. The melancholic, on the other hand, also has a selective perception like the optimist, but he picks the negative aspects instead of the positive ones from the spectrum. The optimist is carried away by hope, the melancholic by concern.[89] The optimist expects the best, the

73

pessimist the worst. Whoever has no big expectations, rarely gets disappointed. Melancholy also involves a view distorted by encouragement. At a higher age and with more life experience, worldly wisdom usually increases and is characterized by more modest hopes. According to Schopenhauer, we tend to brighten up the present by speculating about our favorable chances and imagining hundreds of illusionary hopes, each of which is pregnant with a disappointment if they remain unsatisfied, as usual. Instead we should reflect on all the possible misfortunes, which would partly cause us to take precautionary steps to avoid them, and partly provide pleasant surprises if they do not take place.[90]

> Life presents itself as a continual deception, in small matters as well as in great. If it has promised, it does not keep its word, unless to show how little desirable the desired object was; hence we are deluded now by hope.[91]

At times Schopenhauer seems to ascribe a meaning to life, as if it was meant to teach us a lesson, namely to resign and stop willing.

> With its misfortunes, small, greater, and great, occurring hourly, daily, weekly, and yearly; with its deluded hopes and accidents bringing all calculations to nought, life bears so clearly the stamp of something which ought to disgust us, that

it is difficult to conceive how anyone could fail to recognize this [...].[92]

Schopenhauer distinguishes between daily life with its trifles, and the totality of life in general. Under the aspect of this whole, nothing proves to be worth our efforts, struggles and exertions. All is vain, and "life is a business that does not cover the costs; so that our will may turn away from it."[93]

The life of every individual, viewed as a whole and in general, and when only its most significant features are emphasized, is really a tragedy; but gone through in detail it has the character of a comedy. For the doings and worries of the day, the restless mockeries of the moment, the desires and fears of the week, the mishaps of every hour, are all brought about by chance that is always bent on some mischievous trick; they are nothing but scenes from a comedy. The never-fulfilled wishes, the frustrated efforts, the hopes mercilessly blighted by fate, the unfortunate mistakes of the whole life, with increasing suffering and death in the end, always give us a tragedy.[94]

And even a die-hard optimist would only have to open his eyes to be finally convinced of all the evils in the world. Misery is all around, either evident or lurking in hidden abodes. The hardships, diseases, accidents, bitter needs all belong to the kinds of afflictions life is constantly exposed to. The atrocities committed by man against other men make Schopenhauer agree with Hobbes that "man is a wolf for man". Even worse, everybody is some-body else's "devil". Schopenhauer states that Dante's description of hell fits the world. After all, the material Dante took for illustrating hell is taken from our world.[95]

Schopenhauer sees misery as not only confined to mankind, but everywhere in nature. Every living being sustains its existence by devouring other life forms. Life is always destructive and necessarily at other beings' expense and agony.[96] And this is inevitable. While it is true that things like mountains and valleys, blooms and brooks etc. are pretty to *see*, it is a totally different story to *be* them. As a conclusion, Schopenhauer states the antithesis to Leibniz's thesis that this world is the best of all possible worlds, "This world is the *worst* of all possible worlds."[97] He stresses further that "*optimism*, where it is not merely the thoughtless talk of those who harbor nothing but words under their shallow foreheads, seems to me to be not merely an absurd, but also a really *wicked*, way of thinking, a bitter mockery of the unspeakable suffering of mankind."[98]

Things are bad and they are not getting better. Kant had already rejected the optimism of Leibniz's theodicy and his conviction that pleasure would outweigh pain, and the good would come about by means of the bad. But he had still considered it reasonable to believe in a steady progress towards perfection. Schopenhauer denies the belief that there could ever be a complete cure for evil, pain and grief.

III. On Religion

The Christian trinity of "faith, love, hope" is reflected on by Schopenhauer's highly esteemed predecessor Kant. He bases the legitimacy of hope on the "postulates" of morality which are God, freedom and immortality. He claims that from the categorical imperative to act so that the maxim of one's action could always function as a general rule, reason would allow, or rather demand, the assumption of a justice to come about eventually, namely after death. To guarantee this final justice, free will needs to be presupposed so that we can be held responsible, and a judging God is needed as well as a personal afterlife. Schopenhauer accuses Kant in his "Critique of Kant's Basis of Ethics" of theological concessions, and of making a selfish foundation of morals by still leaving a secret connection between virtue and happiness.[99] Though less obvious than in past theories of happiness, in Kant as well, ethical behavior is rewarded. This threatens to destroy the attitude of pure respect for an unconditioned moral obligation. An anti-moral motive creeps in, namely the selfish hope of going to heaven later. A person therefore does not act purely for the other's well-being, but out of self-interest. This is an ethical dilemma, because for Schopenhauer true morality rests on unselfishness and flows from compassion.

> The egoist feels himself surrounded by strange and hostile phenomena, and all his hope rests on his own well-being. The good person lives in a world of friendly phenomena; the well-being of any of these is his own well-being.[100]

However, feeling pity with everybody may make life harder instead of happier.

Schopenhauer's view on *religion* is shaped by the experience of suffering. So is his philosophy, which not only starts with wonder but also with a "minor chord". All theistic religions with the idea of a good god share the problem of having to answer the question why God allows evil. Whoever loves creation must hate God. Nietzsche observed later that "God died from compassion". This means that belief in God was abolished by men of compassion. Georg Büchner stressed that one can deny evil, but not pain; pain constitutes a gap in creation and is the foundation rock of atheism.[101]

Schopenhauer holds that "who loves truth, hates the gods".[102] All religions are mostly superstitions, and reject reason and science because what they aim at is proclaimed "higher than all reason."[103] Dogmas, rituals, prayers and sacrifices offered to gods, demons or saints feed religious hopes.

> Their service is everywhere closely interwoven with reality, and indeed obscures it. Every event in life is then accepted as the counter-effect of these beings. Intercourse with them fills up half the time of life,

constantly sustains hope, and, by the charm of delusion, often becomes more interesting than intercourse with real beings.[104]

Schopenhauer differentiates between dogmas which can not be rationally understood, and metaphysical propositions which follow a logical structure. While the former may often sound paradoxical, the latter may contain some plausibility. Some moral rules also carry intuitive plausibility. In this sense religion may be an allegory or mythical vehicle for a deeper, true meaning. Schopenhauer stresses that Christianity has something like an outer "shell" and since he wants to get at its content, with which he sympathizes, he breaks the shell.[105] Religion can be truth dressed in a lie. For Schopenhauer, pessimism is on the right track. Pessimism would provide the true inner core of religions.[106] It may sound strange that he considers Christianity as pessimistic. But Schopenhauer means by pessimism in this context that the world is considered as fallen and man as evil.[107] Life appears as if it were a punishment for some guilt. "There seems to me no better explanation of our existence than that it is the result of some false step, some sin of which we are paying the penalty."[108] This is the reason why Schopenhauer sees a kindred spirit among Christianity, Brahmanism and Buddhism.[109] All of these are about some kind of possible salvation from this world of woe and death.

III.1. God

While Kant had claimed the trinity of God, freedom and immortality as indispensable for a moral world order, and main purpose of all metaphysics, Schopenhauer states in his *Manuscript Remains* that the God hypothesis would render impossible the latter two.[110] It is not too difficult to see in which way the assumption of God interferes with freedom. If somebody sins it is because that person is a sinner which falls back on his creator.[111] If there is an omniscient and omnipotent good God, he is responsible for everything and there is no freedom for others in a strict sense.

Schopenhauer's second claim is that God would be inconsistent with human immortality. This thesis is difficult to understand, especially since Schopenhauer does not further elaborate on it. He does give arguments for the finite existence of the body though, including the brain, without which there cannot be consciousness. Also, an immortal soul would be as eternal as its creator, which would reduce the difference between creator and creation. The greatest problem seems to be how eternity should be possible in just one direction. It is weird that our non-existence before we were conceived in our mother's womb does not bother us nearly as much as the idea of our non-existence after death, although both states will probably be identical for us. It is absurd to imagine an eternal consciousness in the future without having had the same consciousness before we came into being.

Man is introduced to the idea of God in early childhood and he normally takes it for granted for a long time, sometimes all his life.[112] However, if one starts to search for corresponding experiences of God, it turns out that God is hidden.

And he is not only hidden but also inconceivable. It is possible to *believe* that the world was created by a personal being, but it is impossible to *think* it. A God is necessarily a personal being. An impersonal God is just an abused word. Personal beings, however, with an individual intellect and will, are known to us exclusively from the animated nature. To assume such an entity as the origin of the world is such a gross idea that it is outrageous to argue that it should go without saying, or that it be an innate idea.[113]

Given the indifference of nature towards our fate, the question arises as to the compatibility of religious dogmas with experience as well as scientific discoveries. But a believer is likely to always find signs and miracles to confirm his belief. For example, if a woman carries a lucky charm and has an accident, she will not conclude that it failed, but claim that it worked by protecting her from something worse.

Similarly, a believer may cling to his belief that nature displays intelligible design and conclude that it was made by an intelligent designer, namely God, even though science can demonstrate how matter is capable of self-organization (*autopoesis*).

Besides mere imitation of rituals and blind acceptance of dogmas, there is another cause for the belief in God, namely existential *fear*. According to Schopenhauer, it is striking to observe that the idea of a living god is mainly supported by harsh weather, especially thunder. This is the most natural "proof of God".[114] It rests on the experience of weakness in view of threats. Being a helpless and exposed creature, man fantasizes a higher being whom he can ask for help. In great distress, in sickness, after bankruptcy or divorce, many people become religious.

Theism is rejected by Schopenhauer. He says that as soon as somebody talks about God, he does not know what he is talking about.[115] Schopenhauer also criticizes the term "atheism" because it suggests that theism is self-explanatory.

Pantheism, where nature is identified with God, is worse. Here again, theism is presupposed. It looks as if the pantheist started with something given called "God" which he did not know what to do with, and therefore identified him with the world. But a God is essentially the opposite of the world.[116] Moreover, the evils of the world are already inconsistent with theism, but even more so with pantheism.[117]

> [Pantheism] assumes that the creative God is himself the world of infinite torment, and, in this little world alone, dies every second, and that entirely of his own will; which is absurd. It would be much more correct to identify the world with the devil [...].[118]

That would be a decent God indeed, whose incarnation is nothing better than this struggling, suffering, bleeding, dying world, where his creatures prey on each other because they can survive only by doing so.[119] Pantheists just give the title "God" to the inner nature of the world, which is unknown to them, and by doing so think they have achieved something.

> But let us merely look at it; this world of constantly needy creatures who continue for a time merely by devouring one another, pass their existence in anxiety and want, and often endure terrible afflictions, until they fall at last into the arms of death. He who has this clearly in view will allow that Aristotle is right when he says: Nature is not divine, but demon-like [...].[120]

All pantheism fails because of ethics.[121] A glance at the world with a moral eye excludes a morally good ruler as well as the godliness of the world.

III.2. Immortality

To make room for a belief in an after-life in order to guarantee a moral world order and justice, an immortal soul must be postulated. "To the hope of immortality of the soul there is always added that of a 'better world'; an indication that the present world is not much worth."[122] Usually when theology combines the belief in God, and in our immortality, as if they belonged together, this is just a thoughtless habit.[123] Schopenhauer states as early as in 1821 that we could only imagine ourselves as immortal insofar we imagine ourselves as eternal, namely as timeless or at least without a beginning. It is weird that we are not concerned about the time before we were born but feel horror about the time when we will no longer exist. It is not the representation of non-existence as such which makes us abhor death, because in that case we would also have to shudder when thinking of the time when we did not yet exist. Certainly non-existence after death is no different than non-existence before life, so it is not more deplorable. However, this is not an idea or thought at all, but the blind drive of the will-to-live, our essence, which causes this *horror mortis*.[124]

If we conceive ourselves as having been created from nothing, it is not far-fetched to fear that we will also return to nothing. Schopenhauer believes that nothing comes from nothing (*de nihilo nihil*) and that something can never become absolutely nothing. It is strange that he does not doubt these statements. Be that as it may, fear of death is universal and not restricted to insight.

> The fear of death is, in fact, independent of all knowledge, for the animal has it, although it does not know death. Everything that is born already brings this fear into the world. Such fear of death, however, is *a priori* only the reverse side of the will-to-live, which indeed we all are.[125]

Schopenhauer assumes that the voice of nature does not lie, and that there is a good reason for the fear of death. What is feared is the destruction of our individuality and, when linked to consciousness, the annihilation of consciousness. This destruction affects the intellect, which is a mere function of the material brain. Schopenhauer refers to the French physiologist Bichat here. Mortal, therefore, are memory, consciousness, perception and sensation.[126] Knowledge, recollections, personality, character, are all destroyed by death. In death there will not be any transition into a different realm of awareness, no final awakening, but the "lantern will be blown out."[127]

Death is the highest resistance which the will, as appearance of the idea of a certain organism, can suffer from matter. Or rather, from lower ideas which are occupying this same matter.[128] With his theory of ideas, derived from Plato, Schopenhauer introduces a backdoor for eternity. For him, a species is an idea stretched out in time. He says that the cat we see playing in the yard is the same as the cat which played there a hundred years ago. Looking back thousands of years or more, however, organisms display less sameness. Schopenhauer confuses slow change with no change, and so he can cling to his opinion of the eternal ideas of species. Since Darwin's revolutionary work *On the Origin of Species* only appeared one year before Schopenhauer's death, he could not deal any more with its challenge to his theory of the metaphysical will. He would have had a hard time with it, too. Schopenhauer still adhered to the theory of Lamarck, who believed that acquired habits were passed on to the offspring. This assumption also encouraged Schopenhauer in his belief in magical power, and of the omnipotence of the will.

The body falls apart after we have passed away, but its elements persist. Matter persists forever. Schopenhauer's contemporaries had a revived interest in Spinoza. In his *Ethics*, Spinoza defined "God or the substance" as that "which is in itself, and is conceived through itself: in other words, that of which a conception can be formed independently of any other conception."[129] Although he used the word God, he identified God with the infinite substance, of which extension and thinking were parallel attributes of one and the same thing. The philosophy professors who gathered around Hegel, and who got paid for fighting against atheism, were fervently discussing the "absolute mind" in an attempt to establish the dominance of mind over matter. While Spinoza had dissolved God in nature, the German idealists interpreted nature as being godly. Schopenhauer replied cynically that if these gentlemen were so desperate for an absolute, he would give them one: It is matter![130] Matter is not made and not perishable, it is truly independent, it is in itself and is conceived through itself, everything springs from it and everything returns to it. What more can be asked of an absolute?

But Schopenhauer does show a more interesting path into eternity. He speaks of the indestructibility of our true essence by death. The will-to-live is the essence of the body, and in itself could be assumed as independent of the forms of knowledge, that is, free of concepts and the forms of intuition, space and time. As such, the will would be timeless. And outside of time, the will would also be free from coming and going. Schopenhauer admits in his *Manuscript Remains* that this is a bold thought though and merely speculative.[131] In his main work, *The World as Will and Representation*, he sounds much more confident. Maybe he was still hoping for a teaching job.

According to Schopenhauer, the soul is a combination of will and intellect, and this combination is split up in death.[132] Unlike Plato and Aristotle, who regarded the will-powered emotions as finite, and rationality as immortal, Schopenhauer attributes immortality to the will. Death separates the intellect from the will, and the will is the immortal part of the soul. The end of the person is as real as the beginning, and we will no longer be that person after death, just as we were not that person yet, before our birth. The person was not his own whole ego, though, but only a manifestation or utterance of an essence which was untouched by the beginning and the ending of such an utterance.[133]

For Schopenhauer, everybody is his own work, and responsible for his intelligible character due to his initial metaphysical choice. We have not been created by God, but we have created ourselves.

This conception is similar to a myth as described in Plato's *Republic* where every man designs himself ideally before birth. The immortal souls reside in the realm of pure ideas and are reincarnated over and over again. But they do not normally remember any of their past lives. It reads as follows:

All the souls had now chosen their lives, and they went in the order of their choice to Lachesis, who sent with them the genius whom they had severally chosen, to be the guardian of their lives and the fulfiller of the choice: this genius led the souls first to Clotho, and drew them within the revolution of the spindle impelled by her hand, thus ratifying the destiny of each; and then, when they were fastened to this, carried them to Atropos, who spun the threads and made them irreversible, whence without turning round they passed beneath the throne of Necessity; and when they had all passed, they marched on in a scorching heat to the plain of Forgetfulness, which was a barren waste destitute of trees and verdure; and then towards evening they encamped by the river of Unmindfulness, whose water no vessel can hold; of this they were all obliged to drink a certain quantity, and those who were not saved by wisdom drank more than was necessary; and each one as he drank forgot all things.[134]

Schopenhauer explains that what sleep is for the individual, death is for the will. The will would get bored with the same toils and routines throughout an infinite amount of time without any real gain, if memory and individuality were retained. So the will-to-live casts them off, drinks from the Lethe, the river of forgetfulness, and then steps out refreshed as a new being. A new day is dawning and new shores are waiting.[135]

Cloudy day at river shore public domain image.[136]

The ego consists of the transitory cognitive part and the eternal willing part. We could thus recognize that we are the original and eternal source of all life: "All of these creatures as a whole are me, and beside me is nothing else" (*Hae omnes creaturae in totum ego sum, et praeter me aliud ens non est*).[137] This state of consciousness where the boundaries of the individual self are disintegrated, accounts for a feeling of serenity. It is a mystical experience of unification with everything around, like merging into the cosmos and becoming one with the ground of the world. It is only then that all personal afflictions lose their bite.

Schleiermacher describes the religious feeling as the feeling of total dependency. It seems that for Schopenhauer, rather, having such access to the world ground and participating in it, causes something like a feeling of reassurance and power. The will to live in us is the same as the principle of life in general, and it is also the principle of the world. Schopenhauer compares the will to the sun being unaffected by changes on earth.

> The earth rolls on from day into night; the individual dies; but the sun itself burns without intermission, an eternal noon. Life is certain to the will-to-live; the form of life is the endless present; it matters not how individuals, the phenomena of the Idea, arise and pass away in time, like fleeting dreams.[138]

Sunburst over a crest of a hill public domain image.[139]

Does Schopenhauer believe in reincarnation? He does not agree with the concept of metempsychosis in Brahmanism, according to which the whole soul as a unity moves into a different body. He sympathizes more with the concept of rebirth or re-creation (*palingenesis*) as it is understood especially in the esoteric teachings of Buddhism. It is, however, a "mystification" because it is impossible to understand how the will would retain its identity after dissolution. And if it does not, it does not make sense to speak of reincarnation. Nevertheless he sometimes seems to offer this prospect as a consolation.[140]

Schopenhauer aims to connect philosophy with science. During his times, natural history was still working with the concept of a "vital force". The concept was already controversial, though. Schopenhauer follows Blumenbach and others and states that whoever denies the vital force, denies his own existence. He identifies this force with the will-to-live, as well as with the kernel of all natural forces.[141] He ascribes to these forces, as their inner essence, that which we perceive in our self-consciousness as our causality, seen from inside. This is the will-to-live.

However, it still remains unclear why the vital force should be eternal. To protect the individual will from being finite, Schopenhauer identifies it with the inner principle in the natural forces as well as the world-will, all of which being located outside of time and space. Schopenhauer considers time and space as merely subjective and linked to consciousness. They would not be properties of the things as they are in themselves. What survives death is not consciousness, but what creates consciousness; neither is it life, but the principle of life, of which life is its appearance.[142]

Schopenhauer must provide reasons to corroborate this statement. The idea of a vital force is connected to the idea of spontaneous generation, the spontaneous origin of life from inanimate matter. Aristotle had assumed such a *generatio spontanea*, which was still widely popular in the 19th century. Schopenhauer was familiar with the work of Johann Baptist van Helmont, *Ortus medicinae* (1648), in which this theory was still uncontroversial. It was only refuted by Louis Pasteur in 1857, three years before Schopenhauer died. This is why Schopenhauer was convinced that "life is certain to the will-to-live". The idea of spontaneous generation had been reinforced by microscopic observations of *infusoria*, minute aquatic creatures which emerged in soaked decomposing vegetative matter.[143] Schopenhauer exclaims that nobody should speak with contempt about matter. Who knows this dust? Take a close look at it: It is able to perform the miracle of creation![144]

But Schopenhauer also realizes that some problems remain unexplained by this theory. It is obvious that the origin of living beings follows certain rules. Moreover, nature does not seem to care about individuals but only species. The restless, powerful urge to mate and propagate, and the resulting huge numbers of germs, is puzzling. It looks as if it was very easy for nature to produce individuals, but extremely difficult to produce a whole species. Why does spontaneous generation only produce known species, never unknown ones? Nature is evidently not able to replace those which have gone extinct, although they had been in her plan. This makes us wonder.[145]

Schopenhauer speaks of a "plan of nature" here, as if nature was a consciously acting subject. However, he rejects teleology in nature. There are purposes in nature, but no intentions.

> The astonished admiration that usually seizes us when we contemplate the endless appropriateness in the structure of organic beings, rests at bottom on the certainly natural yet false assumption that that *agreement or harmony* of the parts with one another, with the whole of the organism, and with its aims in the external world, as we comprehend and judge of it by means of *knowledge*, and thus on the path of the *representation*, has also come into being on the same path; hence that, as it exists *for* the intellect, it was also brought about *through* the intellect.[146]

IV. Rational Hope

Hope always transcends the given. It crosses the factual by a vision of something better, either as world-immanent, that is a hope for worldly goods, or as a transcendent or religious hope for heaven. We shall first discuss the transcendent hope here. The transcendent variety of hope is special because it can not strictly be disappointed, since it cannot be falsified in this life. However, the belief can be lost when it conflicts with knowledge.

In the 17th century a conflict emerged between faith and science which Pascal attempted to solve by acknowledging reasons of the heart (*raisons du coeur*). "The heart has its reasons that reason does not know".

Attempts were also made to reconcile faith and knowledge. In 1793 Kant's work *Religion within the Boundaries of Mere Reason* appeared. Kant strictly separated them and limited knowledge in order to leave room for faith, but also made an effort to rationalize faith. The moral rule shall be more than a matter of taste, and it should be possible for reason to accept an afterlife.[147] Kant denies to man the ability to know his own heart, but along the way to becoming a morally good person, man must be able to *hope* that he can get there by his own effort.[148] In his *Critique of Practical Reason*, Kant says that everybody who is aware of continuously progressing towards this goal out of the moral motive may hope, though not expect for certain, to continue this way in an afterlife. He may hope for an increasing approximation to perfection in an infinite future which is held in God's possession.[149]

Morality does not teach how to become happy, but how to become worthy of happiness. The moral rule tells us to live so that we may deserve God's grace. Only if religion is added, does hope also enter. It is the hope to later harvest bliss in the same measure that we had made efforts to become worthy.[150] Morality becomes fully meaningful only if practical reason postulates three metaphysical ideas, namely God, freedom and immortality.[151] Religious hope is not the basis for action, but it completes action. The determination of an attitude to become a better person results in the rational hope of being rewarded, and of participating in the highest good of the blessed, even, or especially, after death.[152]

To speak of rational hope sounds like a contradiction. Schopenhauer for his part pays no tribute to theology, but evaluates hope afresh. He founds his criticism of hope on the possibility of the reasonable part of man to free himself from the blind will. This includes the emancipation from being determined by others, who would use hope as a means for manipulation. To resist hope is the condition for being so redeemed. Whoever is hoping too much, is trusting too much. Hope lures people to expect some good which never comes, and all the willing people go on dreaming.

> Awakened to life out of the night of un-consciousness, the will finds itself as an individual in an endless and boundless world, among in-numerable individuals, all striving, suffering, and erring; and, as if through a troubled dream, it hurries back to the old unconsciousness. Yet till then its desires are unlimited, its claims in-exhaustible, and every satisfied desire gives birth to a new one. No possible satisfaction in the world could suffice to still its craving, set a final goal to its demands, and fill the bottomless pit of its heart.[153]

In his work *On the Freedom of the Will* Schopenhauer distinguishes thee types of freedom: physical freedom, as absence of material obstacles; moral freedom, as absence of determining motives; intellectual freedom, as absence of error.[154]

Physical freedom is the most immediate and popular use of the term, and easiest to grasp. As soon as somebody, be it a human or an animal, acts according to his own will, whenever he *can* do what he wants, his actions are free in this sense.

The next question, though, is whether somebody can want what he would like to want.[155] This is to ask whether the will is properly free and not necessarily determined by the strongest motive. Schopenhauer quotes from Hobbes' *Moral and Political Works* (1750):

"Nothing takes a beginning from itself; but from the action of some other immediate agent [...] So that, whereas it is out of controversy, that of voluntary actions the will is the necessary cause, and by this which is said, the will is also necessarily caused by other things [...]."[156]

Schopenhauer also agrees with Spinoza's determinism. Spinoza says that if a rock were conscious, and got kicked and flew through the air, it would believe itself to be flying of its own free will. Men are mostly unaware of their causes, and therefore assume that there were none for their acts of will. Schopenhauer denies an empirical "*liberum arbitrium indifferentiae*", which would be to say that an act of will is not necessarily determined by a sufficient cause or reason.[157] All actions follow with strict necessity from an interaction between the individual's character and the strength of his motives.

But Schopenhauer also leans on Kant and acknowledges a so-called "transcendental freedom" which would make it possible to hold people responsible for their deeds. According to this assumption, freedom lies not in what we *do*, but in what and who we *are*. The choice of our intelligible character is thought to be outside of our experience.[158] This is reminiscent of Plato's myth of the souls choosing their fate before birth. But if space and time as the principle of individuation are merely subjective, as are the *a priori* concepts of the understanding, including causality, then the will in itself could be conceived to be free from causality. This is hard to understand because it does not correspond to our experience, and Schopenhauer accordingly cites Malebranche who says that "freedom is a mystery".[159]

The last type of freedom is the intellectual freedom. It is of special concern here in a critique of ideology which aims to shed some light on the connection between knowledge and interest. The intellect is the medium for the motives, and as long as it is in proper working condition, and presents the motives without bias, it can be said to be free in this sense. But the intellect can malfunction, due to drugs for example, or a chemical imbalance in the brain.

The intellectual freedom can also be taken away or reduced by affections of the will, such as emotions and passions. The sudden overwhelming influence of an affect of will renders a fair play among the motives impossible and man either does not know what he is doing, or he is not able to reflect on the consequences of his action, and therefore cannot be held responsible.[160]

Man is not free whenever he is in the grips of hope. Hope functions like a handicap. It deceives him concerning the correct estimate of how likely something is. He remains intellectually impaired as long as he is not able to distinguish unrealistic goals from realistic ones. Reason can become instrumental when its sole criterion is pragmatic value or

103

usefulness. Truth then becomes contingent on preference, and a matter of power playing. The winner is right.

In the presence of hope, man can be guided like a donkey following a carrot on a stick. The donkey is pulling a cart, while the driver is holding a long stick with a dangling carrot in front of the donkey but just out of its reach. The idiom "carrot on a stick" nowadays "refers to a policy of offering a reward for making progress towards benchmarks or goals but not necessarily ever actually delivering.[161] In the case of the "carrot on a stick" motivation, hope is the incentive for action.

Drawing: Rita and Ortrun Schulz

But the surplus of intelligence opens up a chance for freedom. This may be Schopenhauer's last and greatest hope. On the one hand he announces the impotence of reason, on the other hand he attributes to reason the competence to know the ultimate ground of the world. Even more, reason shall provide the means to salvation. Knowledge can set us free from blind willing. It furnishes us with the option to deny the will-to-live, which is the source of all suffering. Reason can realize how the irrational will plays in the show of the universe at its own expense, and can judge and choose for it. A look at the whole may make the motives lose their power. Knowledge can thus become the quieter of the will.

Any state of absence of willing is a blissful state. It can take place through an ascetic lifestyle, or when contemplating or creating a work of art, or observing something without personal interest. Unselfishness is the closest approximation, while still in this life, to a relatively painless condition.

Hope, however, never sleeps and always disturbs the peace of mind by stimulating desire and discontent. In order to soothe hope, it is necessary to restrict the will to the conditions of reason. If the wise man succeeds in this, philosophy may not yield him any profit but may save him from a lot of trouble.

The turning away from life can happen in various stages of sanctification, such as pure contemplation, deeds of compassion and resignation. Resignation can be brought about by mere life experience and may come with age, "hence the countenances of almost all elderly persons wear the expression of what is called *disappointment*".[162] One's own deeply felt suffering is not only a surrogate for virtue, but indispensible for getting us on the right track, and for turning around. Hope for our salvation and deliverance rests more on what we suffer than on what we do.

Since all life is suffering, the equivalent of condemnation consists in eternal life. It would mean participation in all life, and suffering throughout the infinite past, fleeting present, and eternal future. Eternal life would be eternal hell. What life and death teach us is their futility. The sense of life is to gain insight into the vanity of all striving and the transience of everything ever wanted. The purpose of life is – death.

> Just as the whole slow vegetation of the plant is related to the fruit that at one stroke achieves a hundredfold what the plant achieved gradually and piecemeal, so is life with its obstacles, deluded hopes, frustrated plans, and constant suffering related to death, which at one stroke destroys all, all that the person has willed, and thus crowns the instruction given him by life.[163]

Since man has reason and the freedom to choose life or not, "the death of the individual is in each case the unweariedly repeated question of nature to the will-to-live: 'Have you had enough? Do you wish to escape from me?' The individual life is so short, so that the question may be put often enough."[164] If he continues to affirm life, he falls back into nature's womb which means, he is again subjected to the circle of coming and going. The way out of nature can only be determined negatively. It would consist in the absence of all willing. But this condition does not come easy, nor does it tend to persist.

> Even in the case of the individual who approaches this point, the tolerable condition of his own person, the flattery of the moment, the allurement of hope, and the satisfaction of the will offering itself again and again, i.e. the satisfaction of desire, are almost invariably a constant obstacle to the denial of the will, and a constant temptation to a renewed affirmation of it. For this reason, all those allurements have in this respect been personified as the devil.[165]

We have seen that, insofar as Schopenhauer does not give us hope for an eternal consciousness, he does not offer much consolation to most. Only if we resign our individuality, and merge into everything around us, can we hope to find relief from endless suffering. Salvation is possible only if we lose ourselves. The object of *transcendent* hope is – nothing. Schopenhauer's last word in his main work *The World as Will and Representation* is "nothing". When the will freely denies itself, its appearance and the world as its representation, the only hope left is hope for nothing. Schopenhauer sees redemption at the end of a progress from a bad world to a better nothing.

> But we now turn our glance from our own needy and perplexed nature to those who have overcome the world, in whom the will, having reached complete self-knowledge, has found itself again in

everything, and then freely denied itself, and who then merely wait to see the last trace of the will vanish with the body that is animated by that trace. Then, instead of the restless pressure and effort; instead of the constant transition from desire to apprehension and from joy to sorrow; instead of the never-satisfied and never-dying hope that constitutes the life-dream of the man who wills, we see that peace that is higher than all reason [...].[166]

Bibliography

Dictionaries

Handbuch philosophischer Grundbegriffe. Bd. II. Ed. Hermann Krings, H.M. Baumgartner and C. Wild. München: Kösel-Verlag, 1973.
Historisches Wörterbuch der Philosophie. Ed. Joachim Ritter. Darmstadt: Wissenschaftliche Buchgesellschaft, 1974.
Wörterbuch der philosophischen Begriffe. Ed. Rudolf Eisler. Berlin: Mittler & Sohn, [4]1927.

Online Picture Gallery
http://www.public-domain-image.com/

Sources

Aristotle
Aristoteles, *Die Nikomachische Ethik*, transl. and ed. Olof Gigon, München: DTV, [6]1986.
Aristoteles. *Hauptwerke.* Ed. W. Nestle. Stuttgart: Kröner, 1953.

Bloch
Bloch, Ernst. *Das Prinzip Hoffnung.* Werkausgabe Band 5. Frankfurt/M.: Suhrkamp, 1959.

Camus

Camus, Albert. Der *Mensch in der Revolte. Essays.*
Hamburg: Rowohlt, 1953.

Dante

Alighieri, Dante. *Die Göttliche Komödie.* München:
DTV, [6]1992.

Descartes

Descartes, René. *Die Prinzipien der Philosophie.* Transl.
Artur Buchenau. - Hamburg: Meiner, [7]1965.
(Philosophische Bibliothek; 28).
Descartes, René. *Die Leidenschaften der Seele.*
Hamburg: Meiner, 1984. (Philosophische
Bibliothek; 345.)
Descartes, René. *Meditationen über die Erste Philosphie.*
Transl. Gerhart Schmidt. Stuttgart: Reclam,
1983.

Heidegger

Heidegger, Martin. *Sein und Zeit.* Tübingen:
Niemeyer, [11]1967.

Kant

Kant, Immanuel. *Kritik der praktischen Vernunft.* Ed.
Joachim Kopper. Stuttgart: Reclam, 1992.
Kant, Immanuel. *Kritik der reinen Vernunft.* Ed.
Ingeborg Heidemann. Stuttgart: Reclam, 1966.
Reprint 1982.
Kant, Immanuel. *Kritik der Urteilskraft.* Ed. Gerhard
Lehmann. Stuttgart: Reclam, 1963. Repr. 1981.

Kant, Immanuel. *Die Religion innerhalb der Grenzen der bloßen Vernunft*. Ed. Rudolf Malter. Stuttgart: Reclam, 1981.

Lukács

Lukács, Georg. *Die Zerstörung der Vernunft*. 1952. Luchterhand, repr. Neuwied 1962. (Georg Lukács Werke; 9).

Nietzsche

Nietzsche, Friedrich. *Kritische Gesamt-Ausgabe*, ed. Giorgio Colli & Mazzino Montinari, Berlin/New York 1967 ff.

Nietzsche, Friedrich. Zur Genealogie der Moral. *Werke* III. Ed. Karl Schlechta. Repr. [6]1969. Frankfurt: Ullstein, 1979.

Nietzsche, Friedrich. Das Verhältnis der schopenhauerschen Philosophie zu einer deutschen Kultur. In: *Werke* Bd. III. Ed. Karl Schlechta. Frankfurt am Main 1979, pp. 995-998.

Plato

Plato, *The Republic*, around 380 BC, http://everything2.com/title/River+Lethe, by M. Turner, Book X, 2001.

Schopenhauer

Schopenhauer, Arthur. *Gesammelte Briefe*. Ed. Arthur Hübscher. Bonn: Bouvier, [2]1987.

Schopenhauer, Arthur. *Der handschriftliche Nachlaß in fünf Bänden.* Ed. Arthur Hübscher. München: Deutscher Taschenbuch Verlag, 1985.

Schopenhauer, Arthur. *Sämtliche Werke.* Ed. Wolfgang Frh. von Löhneysen. 5 Bände. - Darmstadt: Wissenschaftliche Buchgesellschaft, repr. ²1989.

Schopenhauer, Arthur. *The World as Will and Representation.* Vol. I. Translated from the German by E.F.J. Payne. New York: Dover Publications, 1969.

Schopenhauer, Arthur. *The World as Will and Representation.* Vol. II. Translated from the German by E.F.J. Payne. New York: Dover Publications, 1958.

Schopenhauer Works E-Publications:

http://ebooks.adelaide.edu.au/s/schopenhauer/art hur/essays/chapter9.html, "Psychological Observations" by Arthur Schopenhauer. Translated by Mrs. Rudolf Dircks. © 2014 The University of Adelaide.

http://www.gutenberg.org/files/44929/44929-h/44929-h.htm. Produced by Marc D'Hooghe at http://www.freeliterature.org. *The Basis of Morality* by Arthur Schopenhauer. Transl. by Arthur Brodrick Bullock. Release Date February 16, 2014 [EBook #44929].

http://www.readbookonline.net/readOnLine/225 79/, Arthur Schopenhauer, *On the Sufferings of the World.* Transl. by T. Bailey Saunders.

http://www.readbookonline.net/readOnLine/225
69/, Arthur Schopenhauer, *Religion, A Dialogue Etc: A Few Words On Pantheism*. Transl. by T. Bailey Saunders.

Spinoza

Spinoza, Baruch de. *Abhandlung über die Verbesserung des Verstandes. Abhandlung vom Staate*. Hamburg: Meiner, [5]1977 (Philosophische Bibliothek; 95.)

Spinoza, Baruch de. *Die Ethik; Schriften und Briefe*. Ed. Friedrich Bülow. – Repr. [7]1976. Stuttgart: Kröner, 1982. (Kröners Taschenausgabe; 24).

Spinoza, Baruch de. *Descartes' Prinzipien der Philosophie auf geometrische Weise begründet*. Mit dem „Anhang, enthaltend metaphysische Gedanken". Transl. Artur Buchenau.. Hamburg: Meiner, 1987. (Philosophische Bibliothek; 94).

http://www.gutenberg.org/files/3800/3800-h/3800-h.htm, *The Ethics* - (Ethica Ordine Geometrico Demonstrata), by Benedict de Spinoza, translated from the Latin by R.H.M. Elwes.

Other Works

Barth, Hans. „Schopenhauers ‚Eigentliche Kritik der Vernunft' ". In: *Schopenhauer*. Ed. Jörg

113

Salaquarda. Darmstadt: Wissenschaftliche Buchgesellschaft, 1985, pp. 60-72. (Wege der Forschung; Bd. 602).

Brügger, Peter. „Die radikale Unvernunft der menschlichen ‚Vernunft' – Schopenhauers Beitrag zur Ideologiekritik." *Schopenhauer-Jahrbuch* 66 (1985), pp. 253-257.

Eagleton, Terry. *Ideology: An Introduction*. London/ New York: Verso, 1991.

Fahrenbach, H. *Wesen und Sinn der Hoffnung*. Diss. Heidelberg 1956.

Hasse, Heinrich. *Die Richtungen des Erkennens bei Schopenhauer mit besonderer Berücksichtigung des Rationalen und Irrationalen*. Leipzig: Glausch, 1908.

Hasse, Heinrich. *Schopenhauers Erkenntnislehre als System einer Gemeinschaft des Rationalen und Irrationalen: Ein historisch-kritischer Vergleich*. Leipzig: Meiner, 1913.

Horkheimer, Max. „Die Aktualität Schopenhauers." (1961). In: *Zur Kritik der instrumentellen Vernunft*. Ed. Alfred Schmidt. Frankfurt: Fischer TB, 1985, pp. 248-268.

Hübscher, Arthur. *Denker gegen den Strom. Schopenhauer: gestern – heute – morgen*. Bonn: Bouvier, 1973.

Kerstiens, Ferdinand. *Die Hoffnungsstruktur des Glaubens*. Mainz: Matthias-Grünewald-Verlag, 1969.

Klencke, Hermann. *Pessimismus und Schopenhauer mit Bezug auf Spinoza als Heilmittel des Pessimismus.* Leipzig: 1882.

Kliemt, Hartmut. „Der Glaube als Feind der Aufklärung". In: *Die Lehre des Unheils: Fundamentalkritik am Christentum.* Ed. Edgar Dahl. Hamburg: Carlsen, 1993.

Die Lehre des Unheils: Fundamentalkritik am Christentum. Ed. Edgar Dahl. Hamburg: Carlsen, 1993.

Malter, Rudolf: 'Eine wahrhaft ruchlose Denkungsart': Schopenhauers Kritik der Leibnizschen Theodizee. In: *Studia Leibnitiana* XVIII/2 (1986), pp. 152-182.

Marcel, Gabriel. *Homo viator. Philosophie der Hoffnung.* Düsseldorf: Bastion, 1949.

Marcuse, Ludwig. *Philosophie des Glücks: Von Hiob bis Freud.* Zürich: Diogenes, 1972.

Marcuse, Ludwig. *Unverlorene Illusionen. Pessimismus — ein Stadium der Reife.* München: Szczesny, [2]1966.

Moltmann, Jürgen. *Theologie der Hoffnung: Untersuchungen zur Begründung und zu den Konsequenzen einer christlichen Eschatologie.* München: Kaiser, 1968. (Beiträge zur evangelischen Theologie, Theologische Abhandlungen; 38).

Papst Johannes Paul II. *Die Schwelle der Hoffnung überschreiten.* Ed. Vittorio Messori. Transl. Irene Esters. Hamburg: Hoffmann und Campe, [2]1994.

Pisa, Karl. *Schopenhauer: Kronzeuge einer unheilen Welt.* Wien/ Berlin: Neff, 1977.

Safranski, Rüdiger. *Schopenhauer und die wilden Jahre der Philosophie: Eine Biographie.* Reinbek bei Hamburg: Rowohlt TB, 1990.

Schmidt, Alfred. *Die Wahrheit im Gewande der Lüge: Schopenhauers Religionsphilosophie.* München: Piper, 1986.

Schulz, Ortrun. „Die Kritik der Hoffnung bei Spinoza und Schopenhauer." *Schopenhauer-Jahrbuch* 80 (1999), pp. 125-145.

Schulz, Ortrun. *Schopenhauers Kritik der Hoffnung.* Frankfurt a.M.: Peter Lang, 2002. (Europäische Hochschulschriften, Reihe 20: Philosophie; Bd. 648).

Schulz, Ortrun. *Wille und Intellekt bei Schopenhauer und Spinoza.* Phil. Diss. Hannover 1993. Frankfurt a.M./ Berlin/ Bern/ New York/ Paris/ Wien: Peter Lang, 1993. (Europäische Hochschulschriften, Reihe 20: Philosophie; Bd. 405).

Volkelt, Johannes. „Der Begriff des Irrationalen." *Schopenhauer-Jahrbuch* 8 (1919), pp. 55-93.

Was ist Aufklärung? Kant, Erhard, Hamann, Herder, Lessing, Mendelssohn, Riem, Schiller, Wieland. Ed. Ehrhard Bahr. Stuttgart: Reclam, 1981.

Weimer, Wolfgang. *Die Aporie der reinen Vernunft: Schopenhauers Kritik des Rationalismus.* Diss. Köln 1977.

Weinberg, Steven. „Die Frage nach Gott". In: *Die Lehre des Unheils: Fundamentalkritik am*

Christentum. Ed. Edgar Dahl. Hamburg: Carlsen, 1993.

Windelband, Wilhelm. *Die Geschichte der neueren Philosophie*, Bd. II. Leipzig 1880.

Wren, T.E. "Is Hope a necessary Evil? Some Misgivings about Spinoza's metaphysical Psychology." *Journal of Thought* 7 (1972), pp. 67-76.

Young, Julian. "Is Schopenhauer an Irrationalist?" *Schopenhauer-Jahrbuch* 69 (1988), pp. 85-100.

Index

Notes

[1]*Handbuch philosophischer Grundbegriffe*, ed. Hermann Krings et al., München: Kösel, 1973, p. 693.

[2]Schopenhauer, *Parerga und Paralipomena* II, Psychologische Bemerkungen, § 313 footnote, Löhneysen *Werke* V, p. 688.

[3]Schopenhauer, *Parerga und Paralipomena* II, Einige mythologische Betrachtungen, § 200, Löhneysen Werke V, pp. 486-7.

[4]*Historisches Wörterbuch der Philosophie*, Band 3, ed. Joachim Ritter, Darmstadt: Wissenschaftliche Buchgesellschaft, 1974, pp. 1157ff.

[5]*Historisches Wörterbuch der Philosophie*, Band 3, ed. Joachim Ritter, Darmstadt: Wissenschaftliche Buchgesellschaft, 1974, pp. 1157-1166.

[6]Arthur Schopenhauer, *The World as Will and Representation* II, Chap. XIX, On the Primacy of the Will in Self-Consciousness, New York: Dover, 1958, p. 216.

[7]Aristoteles, *Rhetorik* II, 5, 1382a 21; II, 12, 1389a 20ff.

[8]*Handbuch philosophischer Grundbegriffe*, ed. H. Krings et al., München: Kösel, 1973, p. 692.

[9]Handbuch philosophischer Grundbegriffe, p. 694.

[10]Dante Alighieri, *Die Göttliche Komödie*, München: DTV, 61992. Hölle, III. Gesang, p. 16.

[11]Dante Alighieri, *Die Göttliche Komödie*, Hölle, V. Gesang, p. 26.

[12]René Descartes, *Die Leidenschaften der Seele*, Hamburg: Meiner, 1984, (Philosophische Bibliothek ; 345.), 2. Teil, Artikel 58, p. 99.

[13]Spinoza, Baruch de. *Die Ethik; Schriften und Briefe.* Ed. Friedrich Bülow. – Repr. [7]1976. Stuttgart: Kröner, 1982, p. 126, E3Prop12. Also E3Prop25.

[14]Spinoza, E3, Kröner, p. 132. Cf. the definitions of affects, Kröner, p. 177.

[15]Spinoza, E4Prop47, Kröner, p. 236.

[16]Spinoza, E4Prop47Schol, Kröner, p. 237.

[17]Spinoza, E3Prop50, Kröner, p. 159.

[18]Spinoza, Baruch de. *Abhandlung über die Verbesserung des Verstandes. Abhandlung vom Staate.* Hamburg: Meiner, [5]1977 (Philosophische Bibliothek; 95.) Abhandlung vom Staate (Tractatus politicus) 2/10, Meiner p. 64.

[19]Gabriel Marcel, *Homo Viator: Philosophie der Hoffnung,* Düsseldorf: Bastion, 1949, pp. 71-72.

[20]Ernst Bloch, *Das Prinzip Hoffnung.* Werkausgabe Band 5. Frankfurt/M.: Suhrkamp, 1959, p. 74.

[21]Bloch, ibid., pp. 1-3.

[22]Jürgen Moltmann, *Theologie der Hoffnung: Untersuchungen zur Begründung und zu den Konsequenzen einer christlichen Eschatologie,* München: Kaiser, 1968, p. 16. (Beiträge zur evangelischen Theologie, Theologische Abhandlungen; 38).

[23]Papst Johannes Paul II, *Die Schwelle der Hoffnung überschreiten,* p. 53.

[24]Papst Johannes Paul II, *Die Schwelle der Hoffnung überschreiten,* ed. Vittorio Messori, Hamburg: Hoffmann and Campe, [2]1994, p. 48.

[25]Martin Heidegger, *Sein und Zeit,* Tübingen: Niemeyer, reprint [11]1967, p. 345.

[26]Cf. Albert Camus, *Der Mensch in der Revolte.* Essays, Hamburg: Rowohlt, 1953, pp. 28f.

[27]*Was ist Aufklärung?* Ed. Ehrhard Bahr, Stuttgart: Reclam, 1981, pp. 8-9.

[28]Arthur Hübscher, *Denker gegen den Strom. Schopenhauer: gestern – heute – morgen*, Bonn: Bouvier, 1973, p. 9.

[29]Hübscher, *Denker gegen den Strom*, p. 196.

[30]Hübscher, ibid., pp. 187, 261.

[31]Schopenhauer, *Der handschriftliche Nachlaß*, Band 4/1, Die Manuskriptbücher der Jahre 1830-1852, ed. A. Hübscher, München: DTV, 1985, Pandectae I (1832), Nr. 8, p. 119.

[32]Schopenhauer, *Parerga und Paralipomena* I, Löhneysen Werke IV, title page.

[33]Schopenhauer, „Über Schriftstellerei und Stil", *Parerga und Paralipomena* II, Löhneysen Werke II, pp. 589ff. and „Verhunzung der deutschen Sprache", in: *Der handschriftliche Nachlaß*, Band 4/2: Letzte Manuskripte, ed. A. Hübscher, München: DTV, 1985, pp. 36ff.

[34]Rüdiger Safranski, *Schopenhauer und die wilden Jahre der Philosophie: Eine Biographie*, Reinbek bei Hamburg: Rowohlt TB, 1990, pp. 13 and 14.

[35]Schopenhauer, Arthur. *Gesammelte Briefe*, ed. Arthur Hübscher, Bonn: Bouvier, ²1987, p. 292.

[36]Arthur Schopenhauer, *The World as Will and Representation* II, chapter I, "On the Fundamental View of Idealism", Dover p. 3.

[37]Schopenhauer, *The World as Will and Representation* II, Chapter XIX, On the Primacy of the Will in Self-Consciousness, Dover, p. 206.

[38]Schopenhauer, *The World as Will and Representation* II, Chapter XIX, On the Primacy of the Will in Self-Consciousness, Dover, pp. 201ff.

[39]Max Horkheimer, „Die Aktualität Schopenhauers." (1961). In: *Zur Kritik der instrumentellen Vernunft*, ed. Alfred Schmidt, Frankfurt: Fischer TB, 1985, pp. 250-1.

[40]Cf. Peter Brügger, „Die radikale Unvernunft der menschlichen ‚Vernunft' – Schopenhauers Beitrag zur Ideologiekritik", in: 66. *Schopenhauer-Jahrbuch* (1985), p. 254.

[41]Schopenhauer, *The World as Will and Representation* II, Chapter XV, On the Essential Imperfections of the Intellect, Dover, p. 142.

[42]http://ebooks.adelaide.edu.au/s/schopenhauer/arthur/essays/chapter9.html, "Psychological Observations" by Arthur Schopenhauer, transl. Mrs. Rudolf Dircks. Cf. Schopenhauer, *Parerga und Paralipomena* II, Psychologische Bemerkungen, § 344, Löhneysen Werke V, p. 707.

[43]Wilhelm Windelband, *Die Geschichte der neueren Philosophie*, Bd. II, Leipzig 1880.

[44]Schopenhauer, *The World as Will and Representation* I, The Objectification of the Will, § 24, Dover, pp. 121, 123.

[45]Schopenhauer, *Handschriftlicher Nachlaß* I, p. 234.

[46]Schopenhauer, *Parerga and Paralipomena* II, Über Philosophie und ihre Methode, §9, Löhneysen, p. 15.

[47]http://www.gutenberg.org/files/44929/44929-h/44929-h.htm#CHAPTER_VIc, Schopenhauer, *The Basis of Morality*, transl. Arthur Broderick Bullock, released February 16, 2014 [EBook #44929], pg. 55. Cf. Schopenhauer, *Über die Grundlage der Moral*, Löhneysen Werke III, pp. 746; 760.

[48]http://www.gutenberg.org/files/44929/44929-h/44929-h.htm#CHAPTER_VIc, Arthur Schopenhauer, *The Basis of Morality*, transl. Arthur Broderick Bullock, February 16, 2014 [EBook #44929], pg. 179.

[49]Aristoteles, *Die Nikomachische Ethik*, transl. and ed. Olof Gigon, München: DTV, [6]1986, p. 67.

[50]http://www.readbookonline.net/readOnLine/22579/, Arthur Schopenhauer, *On the Sufferings of the World*, transl. T. Bailey Saunders. Cf. Schopenhauer, *Parerga und Paralipomena* II, Zur Lehre vom Leiden der Welt, Werke V, Löhneysen p. 349.

[51]Schopenhauer, *The World as Will and Representation* II, Chap. XIX, On the Primacy of the Will in Self-Consciousness, Dover, p. 219.

[52]http://ebooks.adelaide.edu.au/s/schopenhauer/arthur/essays/chapter9.html, "Psychological Observations" by Arthur Schopenhauer, transl. Mrs. Rudolf Dircks. Cf. Schopenhauer, *Parerga und Paralipomena* II, Psychologische Bemerkungen, § 313, Löhneysen *Werke* V, p. 688.

[53]Schopenhauer, *Der handschriftliche Nachlaß*, Bd. 3: Berliner Manuskripte (1818-1830), ed. A. Hübscher, München: DTV, 1985, Reisebuch (1820), Nr. 60, p. 19.

[54]Schopenhauer, *The World as Will and Representation* I, Book I, §16, Dover, p. 90.

[55]Schopenhauer, *The World as Will and Representation* I, Book I, §16, Dover, p. 87.

[56]Schopenhauer, *Der handschriftliche Nachlaß*, Bd. 1: Frühe Manuskripte (1804-1818), ed. A. Hübscher, München: DTV, 1985, Nr. 558, p. 377.

[57]Schopenhauer, *Parerga und Paralipomena* II, Zur Lehre vom Leiden der Welt, Löhneysen Werke V, p. 344.

[58]Schopenhauer, *The World as Will and Representation* I, §68, Dover p. 392.

[59]Schopenhauer, *The World as Will and Representation* I, §68, Dover, p. 379.

⁶⁰Schopenhauer, *The World as Will and Representation* I, §
56, Dover p. 310.

⁶¹Schopenhauer, *Der handschriftliche Nachlaß*, Bd. 3:
Berliner Manuskripte (1818-1830), ed. A. Hübscher,
München: DTV, 1985, Adversaria (1829-30), Nr. 215, p.
596.

⁶²Schopenhauer, *Der handschriftliche Nachlaß*, Bd. 1: Frühe
Manuskripte (1804-1818), ed. A. Hübscher, München:
DTV, 1985, Nr. 558, p. 377.

⁶³Schopenhauer, *The World as Will and Representation* II,
Chap. XIX, On the Primacy of the Will in Self-
Consciousness, Dover, p. 217.

⁶⁴Schopenhauer, *The World as Will and Representation* II,
Chap. XIX, Dover, p. 218.

⁶⁵Schopenhauer, *The World as Will and Representation* II,
Chap. XIX, Dover, p. 217.

⁶⁶Schopenhauer, *The World as Will and Representation* II,
Chap. XV, Dover, p. 141.

⁶⁷Schopenhauer, *Parerga und Paralipomena* II, Den
Intellekt betreffende Gedanken, Löhneysen Werke V, p.
81.

⁶⁸Schopenhauer, *The World as Will and Representation* II,
Chap. XXX, On the Pure Subject of Knowing, Dover,
p. 371.

⁶⁹http://ebooks.adelaide.edu.au/s/schopenhauer/arthur
/essays/chapter9.html, "Psychological Observations"
by Arthur Schopenhauer, transl. Mrs. Rudolf Dircks. Cf.
Schopenhauer, *Parerga und Paralipomena* II,
Psychologische Bemerkungen, § 313, Löhneysen Werke
V, p. 688.

⁷⁰Schopenhauer, *The World as Will and Representation* II,
Chap. XIX, On the Primacy of the Will in Self-
Consciousness, Dover, p. 217-8.

[71]Schopenhauer, *The World as Will and Representation* II, Chap. XIX, On the Primacy of the Will in Self-Consciousness, Dover, p. 216.

[72]Schopenhauer, *Parerga und Paralipomena* II, Psychologische Bemerkungen, § 314, Löhneysen Werke V, p. 688. Cf. also Schopenhauer, *The World as Will and Representation* II, Chap. XIX, On the Primacy of the Will in Self-Consciousness, Dover, pp. 220f.

[73]Schopenhauer, *The World as Will and Representation* II, Chap. XXII, Objective View of the Intellect, Dover, p. 280.

[74]Schopenhauer, *The World as Will and Representation* II, Chap. XIX, On the Primacy of the Will in Self-Consciousness, Dover, p. 221.

[75]http://www.public-domain-image.com/art-public-domain-images-pictures/line-art-illustration-pictures/line-art-illustration-of-frog.jpg.html.

[76]Schopenhauer, *Aphorismen zur Lebensweisheit*, „D. Unser Verhalten gegen den Weltlauf und das Schicksal betreffend", *Werke* Band IV, Löhneysen, p. 567.

[77]Schopenhauer, *The World as Will and Representation* II, Chap. XLVII, On Ethics, Dover, pp. 592-3. Cf. also in *Über die Freiheit des Willens*, Löhneysen Werke III, p. 626.

[78]Schopenhauer, *Über die Freiheit des Willens*, Löhneysen Werke III, p. 530.

[79]Schopenhauer, *The World as Will and Representation* II, Chap. XVI, On the Practical Use of Our Reason and on Stoicism, Dover, p. 149.

[80]http://ebooks.adelaide.edu.au/s/schopenhauer/arthur/essays/chapter9.html, "Psychological Observations" by Arthur Schopenhauer, transl. Mrs. Rudolf Dircks. Cf. Schopenhauer, *Parerga und Paralipomena* II,

Psychologische Bemerkungen, § 305, Löhneysen *Werke* V, p. 683.

[81]Schopenhauer, *Parerga und Paralipomena* II, Psychologische Bemerkungen, § 305, Löhneysen *Werke* V, p. 651.

[82]Schopenhauer, *Parerga und Paralipomena* II, Kap. 26, Psychologische Bemerkungen, § 304, Löhneysen Werke V, p. 681.

[83]Schopenhauer, *Parerga und Paralipomena* II, Psychologische Bemerkungen, § 324a, Löhneysen *Werke* V, p. 693.

[84]Schopenhauer, *Parerga und Paralipomena* II, Psychologische Bemerkungen, § 348, Löhneysen Werke V, p. 709.

[85]Schopenhauer, *The World as Will and Representation* II, Chap. XIX, On the Primacy of the Will in Self-Consciousness, Löhneysen Werke II, p. 216.

[86]http://ebooks.adelaide.edu.au/s/schopenhauer/arthur/pessimism/chapter1.html, Arthur Schopenhauer, *On the Sufferings of the World*, transl. T. Bailey Saunders. Cf. Schopenhauer, *Parerga und Paralipomena* II, Zur Lehre vom Leiden der Welt, Löhneysen Werke V, pp. 354-5.

[87]http://ebooks.adelaide.edu.au/s/schopenhauer/arthur/essays/chapter9.html, "Psychological Observations" by Arthur Schopenhauer, transl. Mrs. Rudolf Dircks. Cf. Schopenhauer, *Parerga und Paralipomena* II, Psychologische Bemerkungen, § 312, Löhneysen *Werke* V, p. 687.

[88]Schopenhauer, *Der handschriftliche Nachlaß*, Bd. 3: Berliner Manuskripte (1818-1830), ed. A. Hübscher, München: DTV, 1985, Reisebuch (1822?), Nr. 142, p. 58.

[89]Schopenhauer, *The World as Will and Representation* II, Chap. XIX, On the Primacy of the Will in Self-Consciousness, Dover, p. 280.

[90]Schopenhauer, *Der handschriftliche Nachlaß*, Bd. 3: Berliner Manuskripte (1818-1830), ed. A. Hübscher, München: DTV, 1985, Adversaria (1830), Nr. 215, p. 598.

[91]Schopenhauer, *The World as Will and Representation* II, Chap. XLI, On the Vanity and Suffering of Life, Dover, p. 573.

[92]Schopenhauer, *The World as Will and Representation* II, Chap. XLI, On the Vanity and Suffering of Life, Dover, p. 573f.

[93]Schopenhauer, *The World as Will and Representation* II, Chap. XLI, On the Vanity and Suffering of Life, Dover, p. 574.

[94]Schopenhauer, *The World as Will and Representation* I, §58, The Assertion and Denial of the Will to Live, Dover, p. 322.

[95]Schopenhauer, *The World as Will and Representation* II, Chap. XLVI, On the Vanity and Suffering of Life, Dover, p. 577f.

[96]Schopenhauer, *The World as Will and Representation* I, §58, The Assertion and Denial of the Will to Live, Dover, p. 325.

[97]Schopenhauer, *The World as Will and Representation* II, Chap. XLVI, On the Vanity and Suffering of Life, Dover, p. 583.

[98]Schopenhauer, The World as Will and Representation I, §59, p. 326.

[99]http://www.gutenberg.org/files/44929/44929-h/44929-h.htm#PART_II, pg. 34. Cf. Schopenhauer, *Über die Grundlage der Moral*, II. Kritik des von Kant der

Ethik gegebenen Fundaments, §3 Übersicht, *Werke* III, Löhneysen pp. 642, 643.

[100]Schopenhauer, *The World as Well and Representation* I, §66, Dover, p. 374.

[101]Georg Büchner quoted after Alfred Schmidt, *Idee und Weltwille: Schopenhauer als Kritiker Hegels,* München/Wien: Hanser, 1988, p. 35.

[102]Schopenhauer, *Der handschriftliche Nachlaß,* Bd. 4/1: Manuskriptbücher der Jahre 1830-1852, ed. A. Hübscher, München: DTV, 1985, Spicilegia (1843), Nr. 104, p. 286.

[103]Schopenhauer, *Der handschriftliche Nachlaß,* Bd. 1: Frühe Manuskripte (1804-1818), ed. A. Hübscher, München: DTV, 1985, Nr. 123, p. 77.

[104]Schopenhauer, *The World as Will and Representation* I, §58, Dover, p. 323.

[105]Schopenhauer, *The World as Will and Representation* II, Chap. XLVIII, On the Doctrine of the Denial of the Will-to-Live, Dover, p. 629.

[106]Schopenhauer, *Parerga und Paralipomena* II, Über Religion, § 181, Löhneysen Werke V, p. 459.

[107]Schopenhauer, *Parerga und Paralipomena* II, Zur Ethik, Löhneysen Werke V, p. 251.

[108]http://www.readbookonline.net/readOnLine/22579 /, Arthur Schopenhauer, On the Sufferings of the World, transl. T. Bailey Saunders. Cf. Schopenhauer, *Parerga und Paralipomena* II, Zur Lehre vom Leiden der Welt, Löhneysen Werke V, p. 356.

[109]Schopenhauer, *The World as Will and Representation* II, Chap. XLVIII, On the Doctrine of the Denial of the Will-to-Live, Dover, p. 628.

[110]Schopenhauer, *Der handschriftliche Nachlaß,* Bd. 4/1: Die Manuskriptbücher der Jahre 1830-1853, ed. A.

Hübscher, München: DTV, 1985, Pandectae II (1833), Nr. 66, p. 167.

[111]Schopenhauer, *Der handschriftliche Nachlaß*, Bd. 4/1: Die Manuskriptbücher der Jahre 1830-1853, ed. A. Hübscher, München: DTV, 1985, Pandectae I (1832), Nr. 12, p. 121.

[112]Schopenhauer, *Der handschriftliche Nachlaß*, Bd. 3: Berliner Manuskripte (1818-1830), ed. A. Hübscher, München: DTV, 1985, Adversaria (1829), Nr. 205, p. 591.

[113]Schopenhauer, *Der handschriftliche Nachlaß*, Bd. 3: Berliner Manuskripte (1818-1830), ed. A. Hübscher, München: DTV, 1985, Adversaria (1829), Nr. 229, pp. 614f.

[114]Schopenhauer, *Der handschriftliche Nachlaß*, Bd. 1: Frühe Manuskripte (1804-1818), ed. A. Hübscher, München: DTV, 1985, Nr. 76, p. 40.

[115]Schopenhauer, *Der handschriftliche Nachlaß*, Bd. 4/2: Letzte Manuskripte, ed. A. Hübscher, München: DTV, 1985, Senilia (185354), Nr. 37, p. 12.

[116]Schopenhauer, *Der handschriftliche Nachlaß*, Bd. 4/1: Die Manuskriptbücher der Jahre 1830-1853, ed. A. Hübscher, München: DTV, 1985, Pandectae II (1832), Nr. 12, p. 121.

[117]Schopenhauer, *Der handschriftliche Nachlaß*, Bd. 4/1: Die Manuskriptbücher der Jahre 1830-1853, ed. A. Hübscher, München: DTV, 1985, Pandectae II (1834), Nr. 91, p. 190.

[118]http://www.readbookonline.net/readOnLine/22569 L, Arthur Schopenhauer, *Religion, A Dialogue Etc*: A Few Words On Pantheism, transl. by T. Bailey Saunders.

[119]Schopenhauer, *Der handschriftliche Nachlaß*, Bd. 4/1: Die Manuskriptbücher der Jahre 1830-1853, ed. A.

Hübscher, München: DTV, 1985, Cogitata II (1833), Nr. 147, p. 142.

[120]Schopenhauer, *The World as Will and Representation* II, Chap. XXVIII, Characterization of the Will-to-Live, Dover, p. 349.

[121]Schopenhauer, *Der handschriftliche Nachlaß*, Bd. 4/1: Die Manuskriptbücher der Jahre 1830-1853, ed. A. Hübscher, München: DTV, 1985, Pandectae II (1834), Nr. 91, p. 190.

[122]Schopenhauer, *The World as Will and Representation* II, Chap. XLI, On Death and Its Relation to the Indestructibility of Our Inner Nature, Dover, p. 467.

[123]Schopenhauer, *Der handschriftliche Nachlaß*, Bd. 3: Berliner Manuskripte (1818-1830), ed. A. Hübscher, München: DTV, 1985, Foliant I (1821), Nr. 84, pp. 114f.

[124]Schopenhauer, *Der handschriftliche Nachlaß*, Bd. 3: Berliner Manuskripte (1818-1830), ed. A. Hübscher, München: DTV, 1985, Adversaria (1829), Nr. 207, pp. 592f.

[125]Schopenhauer, *The World as Will and Representation* II, Chap. XLI, On Death and Its Relation to the Indestructibility of Our Inner Nature, Dover, p. 465.

[126]Schopenhauer, *Der handschriftliche Nachlaß*, Bd. 4/1: Die Manuskriptbücher der Jahre 1830-1852, ed. A. Hübscher, München: DTV, 1985, Pandectae I (1832), Nr. 4, pp. 116f.

[127]Schopenhauer, *Parerga und Paralipomena* II, Kap. 10: Lehre von der Unzerstörbarkeit unseres wahren Wesens durch den Tod, § 139, Löhneysen Werke V, p. 322.

[128]Schopenhauer, *Der handschriftliche Nachlaß*, Bd. 3: Berliner Manuskripte (1818-1830), ed. A. Hübscher, München: DTV, 1985, Foliant I (1821), Nr. 26, p. 81.

[129]Spinoza, E1Def3,
http://www.gutenberg.org/files/3800/3800-h/3800-h.htm, *The Ethics*, by Benedict de Spinoza, transl. from the Latin by R.H.M. Elwes.

[130]Schopenhauer, *Der handschriftliche Nachlaß*, Bd. 3: Berliner Manuskripte (1818-1830), ed. A. Hübscher, München: DTV, 1985, Foliant I (1821), Nr. 25, p. 79.

[131]Schopenhauer, *Der handschriftliche Nachlaß*, Bd. 3: Berliner Manuskripte (1818-1830), ed. A. Hübscher, München: DTV, 1985, Foliant I (1821), Nr. 24, p. 79.

[132]Schopenhauer, *Der handschriftliche Nachlaß*, Bd. 4/1: Manuskriptbücher der Jahre 1830-1852, ed. A. Hübscher, München: DTV, 1985, Pandectae (1837), Nr. 190, p. 234.

[133]Schopenhauer, *Der handschriftliche Nachlaß*, Bd. 3: Berliner Manuskripte (1818-1830), ed. A. Hübscher, München: DTV, 1985, Foliant I (1821), Nr. 34, p. 85.

[134]Plato, *The Republic*, around 380 BC, http://everything2.com/title/River+Lethe, by M. Turner, Book X, 2001.

[135]Cf. Schopenhauer, *Der handschriftliche Nachlaß*, Bd. 4/1: Die Manuskriptbücher der Jahre 1830-1852, ed. A. Hübscher, München: DTV, 1985, Pandectae I (1832), Nr. 4, p. 117.

[136]http://www.public-domain-image.com/nature-landscapes-public-domain-images-pictures/coast-public-domain-images-pictures/cloudy-day-at-river-shore.jpg.html.

[137]Schopenhauer, *Der handschriftliche Nachlaß*, Bd. 4/1: Die Manuskriptbücher der Jahre 1830-1852, ed. A. Hübscher, München: DTV, 1985, Pandectae I (1832), Nr. 8, p. 119.

[138]Schopenhauer, *The World as Will and Representation* I, §54, Dover, p. 281.

[139]http://www.public-domain-image.com/nature-landscapes-public-domain-images-pictures/sunshine-public-domain-images-pictures/sunburst-over-a-crest-of-a-hill.jpg.html.

[140]Schopenhauer, *Parerga und Paralipomena* II, Von der Unzerstörbarkeit unseres wahren Wesens durch den Tod, Löhneysen Werke V, p. 328.

[141]Schopenhauer, *Der handschriftliche Nachlaß*, Bd. 4/1: Manuskriptbücher der Jahre 1830-1852, ed. A. Hübscher, München: DTV, 1985, Spicilegia (1843/44), Nr. 113, p. 288.

[142]Schopenhauer, *Der handschriftliche Nachlaß*, Bd. 3: Berliner Manuskripte (1818-1830), ed. A. Hübscher, München: DTV, 1985, Adversaria (1829-30), Nr. 213, p. 596.

[143]Schopenhauer, *Parerga und Paralipomena* II, Zur Philosophie und Wissenschaft der Natur, § 90, Löhneysen Werke V, p. 179.

[144]Schopenhauer, *Der handschriftliche Nachlaß*, Bd. 3: Berliner Manuskripte (1818-1830), ed. A. Hübscher, München: DTV, 1985, Foliant I (1821), Nr. 24, p. 79.

[145]Schopenhauer, *Parerga und Paralipomena* II, Zur Philosophie und Wissenschaft von der Natur, § 72, Löhneysen Werke V, pp. 123f.

[146]Schopenhauer, *The World as Will and Representation* II, Chap. XXVI, On Teleology, Dover, p. 327.

[147]Immanuel Kant, *Die Religion innerhalb der Grenzen der bloßen Vernunft*, ed. Rudolf Malter, Erstes Stück, Allgemeine Anmerkung, Stuttgart: Reclam, 1981, pp. 64ff.

[148]Kant, *Die Religion innerhalb der Grenzen der bloßen Vernunft*, p. 65.

[149]Immanuel Kant, *Kritik der praktischen Vernunft*, ed. Joachim Kopper, Stuttgart: Reclam, 1992, pp. 196f. footnote.

[150]Immanuel Kant, *Kritik der praktischen Vernunft*, p. 206.

[151]Immanuel Kant, *Kritik der praktischen Vernunft*, p. 210.

[152]Immanuel Kant, *Kritik der praktischen Vernunft*, p. 196.

[153]Schopenhauer, *The World as Will and Representation* II, Chap. XLVI, On the Vanity and Suffering of Life, Dover, p. 573.

[154]Schopenhauer, *Preisschrift über die Freiheit des Willens*, Löhneysen Werke III, pp. 521ff.

[155]Schopenhauer, *Preisschrift über die Freiheit des Willens*, Löhneysen Werke III, p. 525.

[156]Schopenhauer, *Preisschrift über die Freiheit des Willens*, Löhneysen Werke III, pp. 598.

[157]Schopenhauer, *Preisschrift über die Freiheit des Willens*, Löhneysen Werke III, pp. 599f.

[158]Schopenhauer, *Preisschrift über die Freiheit des Willens*, Löhneysen Werke III, pp. 622f.

[159]Schopenhauer, *Preisschrift über die Freiheit des Willens*, Löhneysen Werke III, p. 624.

[160]Schopenhauer, *Preisschrift über die Freiheit des Willens*, Löhneysen Werke III, pp. 624ff.

[161]http://en.wikipedia.org/wiki/Carrot_and_stick

[162]Schopenhauer, *The World as Will and Representation* II, Chap. XLIX, The Road to Salvation, Dover, p. 634.

[163]Schopenhauer, *The World as Will and Representation* II, Chap. XLIX, The Road to Salvation, Dover, pp. 637f.

[164]Schopenhauer, *The World as Will and Representation* II, Chap. XLVIII, On the Doctrine of the Denial of the Will-to-Live, Dover, p. 609.

[165]Schopenhauer, *The World as Will and Representation* I, §68, Dover, p. 392.

[166]Schopenhauer, *The World as Will and Representation* I, §71, Dover, p. 411.